Enlightenment
is Not An
Ego Project

Enlightenment
is Not An
Ego Project

Thomas Karl Galten LCSW CSAC

Enlightenment is Not An Ego Project

Copyright © 2018 by Thomas Karl Galten

ISBN 978-1-935914-81-5

Cover and Interior design by River Sanctuary Graphic Arts

Printed in the United States of America

Additional copies available from:
www.riversanctuarypublishing.com
amazon.com and other online retailers

River Sanctuary Publishing
P.O Box 1561
Felton, CA 95018
www.riversanctuarypublishing.com
Dedicated to the awakening of the New Earth

All thanks and gratitude
to the One Self, the Supreme,
who we each ultimately are

Contents

❄

Preface

It seems to me critical, perhaps especially when writing in the spiritual genre, to pay close attention to the meanings and connotations of words and language. Therefore, for the purposes of clarity and, hopefully, the avoidance of confusion, I will here briefly highlight a few points.

First, this text employs a number of terms which, in that they each point or refer to the ultimate dimension, should be understood as essentially synonymous. I thus use the words Tao, Brahman, the Self and God with an essential interchangeability. Even the words consciousness and awareness – though their respective meanings are distinguishable in much esoteric spiritual writing – have the same basic meanings in this text, as will be clear.

Similarly, after some consideration of the issue, I have chosen to capitalize words sparingly. That is, while, for example, the word "God" and the phrase "ground of being" point to the same dimension, only words that have traditionally been capitalized (such as Brahman, Tao, Atman, the Self) are capitalized in this book. I have not, therefore, capitalized more obscure and less traditional terms which no less unequivocally also point to the ultimate (such as the light, the one, the formless, etc). So too, following Carl Jung and others, the term "self," when it appears in this text with a lower case "s," refers to the ego (or person). When it appears with a capital "S," it refers to the universal one Self.

Finally, all quotes from the Bible are taken from *The New Oxford Annotated Bible, Revised Standard Version.*

1

❄

Introduction

Enlightenment. It seems so many of us want it today. You, by picking up this book, identify yourself as being, in all probability, one of us.

Perhaps you've come to view yourself as a spiritual seeker. Maybe you've been on the path for many years. Or maybe you feel that you've just started out.

It is probable that you have suffered considerably. Seekers often have. Perhaps you're the product of an alcoholic or otherwise dysfunctional family. Maybe you're a survivor of childhood abuse of some types(s) or form(s). Or maybe you're a recovering alcoholic, sex or drug addict, compulsive gambler, food-a-holic or addicted to something (or someone) else or maybe even all of the above. You might be a member of a Twelve Step program and, in the spirit of Step 11, you're seeking to improve your conscious contact with the God of your understanding.

On the other hand, maybe you feel you've been living a pretty normal and ordinary life. And yet, you are sensing a lure in a new, inward and spiritual direction. Your restlessness compels your search for "something," you know not what.

You might be a religious believer in a more or less conventional sense, a member in good standing of your parish, mosque, synagogue or temple community. You might have attended private, religiously sponsored schools, been baptized, confirmed and married in the church or otherwise have followed closely the traditions of your religion.

Or you might have done all of this earlier in life and have since fallen away from an active religious life. Maybe you have even become disillusioned with the doctrines you were taught, believing them now to lack credibility, experiential verification or to be ineffective at satisfying your spiritual hunger.

Still others who pick up a book such as this have never professed religious belief of any type and were raised in non-religious households. Yet, such an individual can come to feel embraced or grasped by he-knows-not-what. And now he's on a search for this elusive dimension which has come to him largely unbidden.

Whatever your past, your life situation at present, your age, gender, socio-economic background, vocation, culture or any other demographic category we use to sort out human beings, you would not be reading these words if you hadn't concluded – consciously or less so – that the rewards which the world, including the people most near and dear to you, can provide simply will no longer suffice or satisfy ultimately.

So far so good. You get what I'm saying. But right now you may be asking the following questions: What is it I'm looking for? How do I get it? How will I know when I've found it? How can a book – this one or any book – promote my finding that for which I search?

Good questions. And quite understandable questions. This book has been written, in fact, in response to these, and other, questions which have occurred to me on my own journey and which have been asked by many others with whom I have worked as a psychotherapist and clinical substance abuse counselor.

The present book is a fairly simple presentation. It is neither primarily theological nor philosophical in nature, though ideas typically thought of as theological, esoteric, philosophical, mystical or religious are used to help explain, clarify, illustrate or point to the experience for which you are seeking.

For I can tell you this with certainty: You are not searching for ideas, novel ways of describing reality, a new philosophy or religion, information that can be considered or analyzed by the thinking mind or someone or something that can be objectified and known apart from yourself. Instead, you are looking for an experience.

Similarly, the transformation of consciousness that is, I assure you, already underway in, by and through you entails not merely the adoption of a new worldview, an improved approach to human relationships, more positive thinking patterns, better social role functioning or less emotional distress, though all of these phenomena are certainly implied by the transformation. Moreover, though I am neither putting down nor criticizing ideas (indeed, this fairly small book contains many of them), I *am* convinced that only a personal realization, and not ideas, will fully satisfy the spiritual seeker. In short, you want to actually *feel* connection, peace and deep fulfillment. You are searching, once again, for an experience.

So if we can agree from the start that only something "beyond words and ideas" (or, if you prefer, "prior" to words and ideas) can ever fully relieve your discontent and settle your restlessness, we can move on to a discussion which will, in its synergistic relationship with the spiritual energy that you as the reader bring to it, provide illumination and boost your ongoing transformation. Because, whether you realize it or not, the fact that you have begun reading this book – I will say again – is a sure and certain indicator that transformation of consciousness has begun in you.

As Alan Watts wrote:

> *For as soon as the Self begins to will the end of the ego-conscious stage, the ego becomes inflamed with a passion for God, or for metaphysical knowledge...The very fact that a person begins to be interested in the spiritual life, in realization, in union with God, is a certain sign that the process of awakening has begun....Thus when anyone...begins to think of God, to practice any spiritual exercise, or to desire realization, he is expressing the will of the Self. Were this not so he could neither want nor be able to do it.[1]*

And please be assured that what has begun in you, though perhaps perplexing, is ultimately creative. You are neither disintegrating nor going mad. Neither – despite what you might have heard from the mental health establishment – are you sick, disturbed or suffering from a "disorder" which must be "treated" by an expert (though some counselors and psychotherapists do understand the spiritual transformation process and can be quite helpful). In the spirit, then, of Carl Jung's admonition that no teacher can take the seeker further than she herself has gone, choose wisely who would assist you and measure their effectiveness by way of your own experience.

Finally, this book should be understood as a dialogue with the reader. I have no interest whatsoever in advice-giving or in telling anyone what "must be done" or avoided to "get this spiritual thing right." Such an approach would lack faith or trust in the process and represent an ultimately futile "outside-in" approach to what is essentially an "inside-out" process in that nothing which does not come directly from within yourself will ever be liberating or sustainable. So look within, not to me or to anyone else. You are in the midst of a genuine transformational process which, now that it has begun, will not stop.

Yet, despite the undeniably individualistic or personal dimension of transformation, none of us need be alone in it, either. That's where I and others who've had – and are having – essentially the same experience as you are having may be helpful. Just as a woman in labor is physically able to give birth alone, most women understandably prefer to have a helper(s) – such as her partner, a physician, nurse or midwife, for examples – present to ease things along, be encouraging and to join with her in the process of giving birth. In my work as a psychotherapist who takes spirituality seriously, I regard myself as a sort of "spiritual midwife," present in order to be of whatever help I can be in the birth of the Self by and through humans. But, as is true of the literal midwife and childbirth, I neither cause spiritual pregnancies to occur nor do I initiate the labor process as the Self begins to emerge; those things happen by themselves (or, if you prefer, by the grace and will of God, which means the same thing). But I am there to assist and to hopefully facilitate the event.

So let's move forward with this exploration and first take a closer look at what apparently "ails you," so to speak – that is, an acute thirst for spiritual experience – which usually issues in varying measures of restiveness and discontent. This thirst is what some have called a search for God and others have called the Self's search for itself.

---

[1] Watts, Alan (1972). *The Supreme Identity,* pp. 172-173.

✿

Chapter 1

What do You Want?

I often ask persons who come in for counseling, "What do you want?" Generally speaking, people understand the question and respond quite earnestly.

"I want to be happy." "I want my life to be better." "I want peace." "I want my marriage/family life to improve." All very valid – and entirely legitimate – answers to my question.

And so, similarly, I ask this question now of you who have picked up this book: "What do you want? In particular, what are you looking for in this book?"

Many readers would reply in much the same way as counseling clients do: "I want to deepen my spirituality." Or: "I want the peace and serenity that I believe this book is offering the reader." Again, these are valid and reflective responses.

Yet, at the risk of offending the reader, I will state here that these answers also expose a common, almost universal, lack of awareness – the awareness that you *already have* that for which you seek. Even more specifically, that you *already are* that for which you seek.

"What do you mean?" you might ask. Simply this: The personal experience of peace which you may believe you lack (or wish more of) is, paradoxically, found only when the searching phenomenon (or "the seeker") consciously, and in full subjectivity, "comes together," so to speak, with itself. As Dennis Waite has written:

We spend all our efforts looking outside of ourselves for...
lasting happiness. Yet it is the act of looking that takes us
away from happiness.[1]

This coming together with oneself, or "Self-realization," as it is sometimes called, can also be described as a re-direction of energy – energy which had been directed "out and away" from the seeker in a compulsive search for completion, is now "contained," we might say, and so generates consciousness of itself. "Consciousness becoming conscious of itself," as the 20th century Indian sage, Nisargadatta Maharaj, often put it, is the omega point, the true end of the search. The searcher has realized that she has unknowingly been seeking for the deepest aspect of her own very self – which is ultimately the Self or the experience of being aware – all along.

"So why read this book?," you ask. Another good question. If you are asking this question right about now then I would say to you: "You're getting the point."

No book, after all, is actually necessary for awareness to become aware of itself. No book is the source of the experience of connection and deep integrity you seek, just as no counseling regimen or counselor is the source of peace, happiness, contentment or joy.

On the other hand, perhaps this book can act as a sort of catalyst and promote Self-realization in ways similar to that of a good counseling relationship. Might this book be a teacher for you in helping to point you toward – or identify you with – the realm you seek? My hope is that it does just that.

But if this book is to function for you in this manner, you must view it as a relative pointer to the absolute. The way I describe things here can be described in other, perhaps better, ways. Moreover, you may not fully grasp, or agree with, everything I say.

No matter. This book does not stand on its own. As noted in the "Introduction," the present work is neither a philosophical argument nor is it primarily an attempt to convey information or theory. It is mainly a signpost pointing at the dimension of yourself for which you are seeking. As a signpost, it undoubtedly has its flaws and imperfections and is not itself that dimension of consciousness. Read it, if you will, in a spirit of openness and willingness and I am confident that it will benefit you, just as counseling inevitably benefits those clients who are willing and open to experience a true and authentic relationship with a counselor capable of genuineness, presence, empathy and unconditional positive regard.[2]

But what do we mean by "direct experience"?

---

[1] Waite, Dennis (2003). *The Book of One: The Spiritual Path of Advaita*, p. 59.

[2] Carl Rogers posited, beginning in the 1950's, that what he termed the three "core conditions" of psychotherapy – the genuineness of the therapist, the therapist's empathy and his capacity for unconditional positive regard – constituted the "necessary and sufficient" elements of successful psychotherapy. He then spent 30 years rigorously researching his hypothesis and, to this day, psychotherapy outcomes research conducted by numerous researchers and clinicians consistently upholds Rogers' claims that the quality of the therapeutic relationship is the largest factor in positive client change. Toward the end of his life, Rogers suggested that a fourth condition, the "presence" of the therapist – by which he implied a specifically spiritual quality of transparency to the deepest levels of oneself – can also greatly strengthen the positive impact of psychotherapy.

❋

Chapter 2

Spiritual Experience or the "Knowledge of God"

What, indeed, is meant by the phrase "direct experience" in the spiritual context? Let's address this issue by first ruling out what I do *not* mean by it. I do not, for instance, propose that you lack a proper belief system. In other words, it's not that I or anyone else has a new or better set of philosophical, psychological or theological tenets the incorporation of which into your worldview will bring you peace. If that were the case, simple intellectual assent to doctrine of some type or another would do the trick. But belief in, or intellectual assent to, doctrinal statements of any type – as you might already know – simply does not yield the desired effect.

My assertion that you are not looking for a new belief system may seem almost too obvious to mention here. But in even a brief survey of the history of religion and philosophy – two disciplines by which humanity has sought to answer its most compelling questions – we encounter considerable emphasis upon reason, along with doctrinal, creedal and faith claims that are inevitably abstract in their expression. And language-based abstractions from experience cannot satisfy the restless soul. It appears, in fact, that humanity is now realizing the limits of conventional philosophy and religion and must therefore go beyond them.

So too, neither am I suggesting that you lack knowledge in the sense of empirically or theoretically-based information that can be passed on from one mind to another. Simply, for example, my telling you that "you have everything, or are everything, already and so don't actually need to find anything more or other than what is happening now" – however verifiably true that statement, as we will see, is – cannot constitute the experience which you must yourself undergo personally or "from within," we might say.

What's more, by "experience" I am not referring to phenomena of the senses – sometimes referred to as "the outer world," as in what can be seen, heard, touched, etc. After all, if the realm of the senses could satisfy in any final or ultimate sense you would not be reading this book.

Yet, neither am I referring to what some would call the "inner world" nor our "inner experience" if by the adjective "inner" is meant the realm of thought and emotion. For, like sense-based experience, thought and emotion occur closer to what might be called the "surface" of consciousness and so lack the capacity to satisfy depth-level spiritual thirst.

Instead, spiritual searching can only be satisfied by spiritual, or what Immanuel Kant, Ralph Waldo Emerson and others have called "noetic," or transcendental, knowledge, which is of a different order than sense and reason-based knowledge. Richard M. Bucke used the term "cosmic consciousness" to describe this dimension of knowledge. Whereas sense and reason-based knowledge might be characterized as "outside-in" knowledge – that is, knowledge that is mediated by the senses or the mind – spiritual knowledge comes, as already implied above, by way of the intuition, or from the "inside-out."

William James wrote in his classic, *The Varieties of Religious Experience:*

...mystical states seem to those who experience them to be also states of knowledge. They are states of insight into depths of truth unplumbed by the discursive intellect. They are illuminations, revelations, full of significance and importance, all inarticulate though they remain; and as a rule they carry with them a curious sense of authority.....when the characteristic sort of consciousness once has set in, the mystic feels as if his own will were in abeyance, and indeed sometimes as if he were grasped and held by a superior power.[1]

Now the term "spiritual knowledge" is synonymous and entirely interchangeable with a number of somewhat commonly used words and phrases, such as: enlightenment, knowledge of the infinite or the divine, mystical or esoteric knowledge, gnosis, knowledge of or union with God, cosmic consciousness, spiritual insight and depth-level awareness, among others. Aldous Huxley referred to the central core of teachings which have proceeded from out of this profound experience as the "perennial philosophy" in that the experience has been described in all times, places and cultures since the dawn of human history.

Moreover, unlike rational and empirical knowledge, spiritual knowledge implies what Eckhart Tolle and others have termed a "transformation of consciousness," which refers to a shift, most often gradual, in the way one perceives and experiences oneself and the world. Transformation of consciousness also implies what has above been referred to as Self-awareness or Self-realization and has implications for every aspect of one's experience – cognitive, emotional, interpersonal, physical and behavioral.

Transformation of consciousness, then, is fundamentally a spiritual experience which "comes up," so to speak, from "deep within." It is what you have been desiring, mostly without consciously realizing it. Moreover, this shift in consciousness, effected as it is by knowledge of (or direct contact with or identification with) the infinite (which is the deepest aspect of yourself), is, as stated above, an intuitively mediated realization of deep spiritual truth and was referred to by James as a rebirth. Certain humans, as he pointed out, "must be twice-born in order to be happy"[2]. They must, in other words, be made new selves.

The metaphor of the new self is common in spiritual teachings and literature and is found, for examples, in the New Testament writings of St. Paul and is implied in Vedanta (usually described as a school of teaching within Hinduism founded by early 9th century teacher, Adi Shankara) by the insight that "Atman (the divine within) is Brahman (the universal consciousness within which all form exists); and Brahman is Atman. Between the two, there is no difference."

It is important, of course, to distinguish between "spiritual experience" or "spiritual knowledge," on the one hand, and "spiritual teaching," on the other hand; the latter is the *description* of spiritual experience and knowledge. Spiritual teachings are attempts to, as effectively as possible, better acquaint learners or seekers with that dimension of themselves – called by Rudolph Otto "the numinous" – out of which spiritual experience emanates.

Spiritual experience, on the other hand, is, wrote Otto, "ineffable....in the sense that it completely eludes apprehension in terms of concepts"[3] – that is, though words, language and ideas can "point" or refer to it, none of these can contain or capture the essence of spiritual experience, nor can they be used to create or to cause the spiritual experience to occur (or to permanently stave it off, for that matter). This book, then, as is true of all spiritual books, represents spiritual teaching, not spiritual experience itself.

So just what is the content of this experience to which we are attempting to point? The answer to this question, key as it is to understanding the thesis of this text, is actually quite remarkably and surprisingly simple. The ultimate spiritual experience, enlightenment, is simply coming to know one's true identity as the awareness (or consciousness) that underlies all phenomena. I am, in other words, not the time and space-bound apparent "person" named "Karl," who, "inhabiting" a human body, has a personal history and will one day die. I am, instead, *that which is aware* of this body, along with these particular thinking, emotional and behavioral patterns – indeed, I am what is aware of all form. I am thus timeless and spaceless awareness.

---

[1]   James, William (1958). *The Varieties of Religious Experience*, p. 293.

[2]   ibid, p. 140.

[3]   Otto, Rudolph (1958). *The Idea of the Holy*, p. 5.

✿

Chapter 3

How Do I Satisfy My Spiritual Thirst?

To briefly summarize: In the preceding two chapters I have made the claim that the reader is searching for a spiritual experience and have, to some extent, described the essence of that spiritual experience.

Yet, the reader, at this point, might very well be wondering, as have so many sensitive seekers with whom I have had the privilege to work over the years: "All of this teaching perhaps makes some sense as theory or esoteric philosophy. But how do I go about satisfying this thirst I apparently have for the divine, for God, for my deep Self or whatever you want to call it? That spiritual experience about which you speak is what I want. How do I get that?"

These are probably inevitable questions. I have myself asked these same questions. And if I am to subscribe to my own statements above regarding the utter ineffectiveness of the mind and of sense-based experience in bringing about spiritual transformation, then I must acknowledge this ineffectiveness to be equally true of the teaching I have here briefly articulated.

Thus it is that we must face the issue directly: Why is it, even after having given intellectual assent to statements describing what appears to be plausible truth, that we are still not getting what we want? Or, as a therapy client asked me recently, "Why is it so difficult to awaken and, once awake, to stay awake?" Borrowing an analogy from Eckhart Tolle, we might ask, "If all I can do is study honey but not, by my own effort, actually *taste* honey, then how does tasting come about?" So let's examine this issue of directly experiencing what we have, up to this point, only been describing.

First, we would probably all agree that to ask the question, "How do I get this?" is proof beyond doubt that the questioner believes herself to be insufficiently enlightened. Why else would she be asking the question "How can I become enlightened (or more enlightened)?" It is also safe to assume that the questioner believes that an experience called "enlightenment" – or "becoming conscious of consciousness" to, once again use the words of Nisargadatta Maharaj – will bring her peace, contentment and maybe even unending bliss.

And so, as Jiddu Krishnamurti often pointed out, one inevitably seeks out methods, techniques and exercises – preferably endorsed by a wise guru or teacher – that one hopes will capture the long-sought-after prize for oneself. This strategy is understandable. The market, we might say, in enlightenment is assumed to respond to those most willing to put forth the requisite effort and to take risks. Indeed, we tend to view enlightenment as a product or commodity governed by the same capitalistic forces as are all other commodities.

But, as Jeff Foster writes:

Liberation is not something that an individual can get, like he can get a nice suntan, or a bigger bank balance, or a shiny new sports car. It's not something a person can achieve like he can achieve a high score in an IQ test.
It's not something that can be reached through effort, or persistence, or luck, or anything else.[1]

Let's further consider the apparent impossibility of achieving enlightenment, a position taken by the great teachers of all times and traditions. If, after all, desiring enlightenment, and so acting on that desire, is futile, we'd best determine whether or not everything we've been doing in order to achieve enlightenment has, in the end, been for naught.

In fact, maybe we have inadvertently been putting enlightenment even further out of reach. Perhaps the ancient Zen master, who said "By their very efforts to get it they lose it," was speaking critical, if subtle, truth. If so, we are forced, it seems, to view spiritual awakening as being fundamentally different from anything else which we may wish to attain in this world. Might spiritual awakening be the one phenomenon which does not respond to the law of effort and attainment in that it cannot be gotten? Might it be, indeed, that the harder one tries the more out-of-reach it becomes? This, I believe, is what David R. Hawkins was referring to when he wrote:

> *Whereas ordinary mental functioning could be*
> *typified as a constant effort to 'get' something, spiritual*
> *realization is totally effortless, passive and spontaneous.*
> *It is received rather than obtained...One cannot get it*
> *by effort or endeavor...That which is formless cannot be*
> *manipulated.*[2]

If these things be true of spiritual experience, then our world is turned upside-down and common sense is turned inside-out. After all, here we are confronted with truth so perplexing that we may need to re-think deeply unconscious assumptions we have long held about ourselves – perhaps even including our very identities.

Let's explore further.

1   Foster, Jeff (2007). *Beyond Awakening: The End of the Spiritual Search,* p. 19.

2   Hawkins, David R. (2011). *Dissolving the Ego, Realizing the Self: Contemplations from the Teachings of David R. Hawkins;* edited by Scot Jeffrey, p. 64.

❀

Chapter 4

Desire

As was implied above, then, we spiritual seekers find ourselves
wanting, or desiring, enlightenment in the same way that we perhaps once desired a new toy, a fancier car, a bigger house, a stronger
body, a more attractive partner, a better job or other forms in this
world. Yet, didn't the Buddha, in his Four Noble Truths, identify
the phenomenon of desire (or "tarsa" in the original Sanskrit) as
the source of human suffering? The teaching that desire is the
source of suffering clearly represents a reversal of the way we tend
to view spiritual fulfillment in that we generally regard desire, not
only as indicating lack of the desired object, but also as providing
the drive which will be necessary to achieve it. In other words, we
reason: "How am I to achieve anything if there is no motivation
(or desire) to achieve it?"

I am, as a psychotherapist, particularly reminded here of the
work of the great systemic family therapists such as Jay Haley,
Salvador Minuchin, Carl Whitacker and Virginia Satir, among
others, who pointed out that it is not a family system's problems,
as such, that bring them to therapy. Instead, it is the efforts the
system makes in attempting to solve its problems – which only make
them worse and, in fact, only adds another layer of dysfunction
onto the original dysfunction – that frustrates the family enough
to seek help.

Similarly, many of us have tried numerous approaches and practices to attain the desired goal of peace, serenity, and spiritual fulfillment. Meditation of various types. Authors and teachers. Different religions or none at all. And this is not to mention the identifiable addictions and compulsions which some of us fell into on our unconscious search for connection, union and peace.

We are thus obviously caught in a self-perpetuating cycle of attempting to attain something that our desire-driven attempts are themselves blocking us from having. Yet, to consciously and deliberately attempt the quelling of desire and the efforts it inspires represents more desire. Now, for all the world, I am desiring not to desire!

In other words, that elusive sense of deep connection and the overcoming of inner dividedness that you cannot seize hold of and keep by way of effort can neither be achieved nor held by *not* attempting to seize it. Both activity and passivity are thus futile as both are purposeful strategies, driven by desire and invested in a future outcome abstracted from the formal content of the present moment. "By their seeking for it they produce the contrary effect of losing it…for that is using mind to seek mind."[1]

The dilemma thus apparently has no solution on its own level as any attempt at resolution inevitably results in endless feedback loops, as Gregory Bateson, Paul Watzlawick, Ludwig von Bertalanffy and other systems theorists have shown. Just as a thirsty person who drinks salt water in hopes of relieving her thirst will only become more thirsty, the seeker who seeks peace by way of purposeful methods only becomes more discontent. Resolution obviously must come, therefore, if it is to come at all, from another level, realm, or dimension of consciousness than the thinking and willing mind.

What realm is this? Chapter 2 has already provided an answer to this question. But if we cannot access this level by way of goal-directed acts, decisions or choices of the will, are we doomed to suffer, trapped in a human condition which we cannot substantially change and over which we have no control?

That second question, which represents the one all seekers ask, is more compelling than that of naming, speculation, abstractions of all types or theorizing. It is probably the seeker's central question as the answer seems to promise the possibility of liberation.

Thus it is to this question that we must now turn.

---

[1] Huang-po in "Treatise on the Essentials of the Doctrine of Mind"; cited in Watts, Alan (1989); *The Way of Zen*, p. 99.

❖

Chapter 5

Is there a Way Out of the Trap?

If the unsolvable dilemma described above pretty much sums up your life at this point, then you may be asking, in addition to the questions asked at the end of chapter 4: "Then how can I have the 'peace which passes all understanding' that the teachers talk about?" But now, even as you ask the question, you might be realizing that your very asking of the question indicates your bondage to a hopeless conundrum that simply cannot, as shown above, be resolved on its own terms. "But if I can't get it because I want it" you continue, "and I can't stop wanting it without falling into further wanting, the whole thing sounds hopeless."

Is there a way out of the dilemma? The reader, if she has grasped the essence of the futility described above, will at this point be able to answer unequivocally: "No, there is obviously no way out of this trap." In other words, there is nothing that you, conceived as an individual, can do. There's no formula the mind can conjure up. No steps or techniques to follow that will win you the peace and depth sense of wholeness, wellbeing and harmony for which you as a seeker yearn. It simply cannot be done. Just as a non-swimmer who falls into deep water may desperately hope that his frantic struggle will save him from drowning, the spiritual seeker goes this way and that, tries this method and that, this approach and that – ultimately to no avail. In fact, just as the drowning person's struggle only increases the likelihood of actually drowning, the efforts of the seeker only increase her anxiety, thus reinforcing the condition she wishes to escape.

If you're thinking like this or – even better – if you're actually *feeling* your lack of effectiveness, then you're clearly coming up against a fundamental fact of your existence. And you are thus closer to the kingdom of heaven than you realize.

Let's once again briefly summarize the situation: You – or at least the supposed individual with a name, a body, a mind and a history that you take yourself to be – cannot attain what you most desire. It's not that you simply haven't found the right teaching yet. It's not that you're doing something wrong or not doing what you should be doing. It's not that you haven't been on the spiritual path long enough. You haven't reached the omega point of spirituality for the consummately simple reason that it cannot be done.

The mind (or ego) rebels at this notion of powerlessness. It seems to run counter to the messages most of us modern people have heard all of our lives: If you work hard you will succeed.

This is decidedly *not* to say that there isn't at least some relative truth to the "gospel of can-do achievement." If you honestly look around yourself and observe outcomes in your own life and the lives of others you'd probably conclude that hard work, goal-setting and determination are quite highly correlated with success in this world. Moreover, there is neither anything "wrong" with success in this world nor is there anything wrong with desiring success in this world. Furthermore, success in this world and spiritual realization are not mutually exclusive. But they do happen, we might say, at different levels. As Eckhart Tolle has said, *You can achieve many things by way of effort except what is of absolute importance.*

Indeed, even "letting go and letting God," a favorite Twelve Step program slogan, when understood as a decision or an attitude, further binds us as to "let go" is itself an attempt, however subtle, to escape one's current experience in the moment and thus represents a stance of non-acceptance and an affirmation of ego (which, as will see, is an assumption of separation). Since to truly let go, or to surrender, represents not a choice but a collapse – which, of course, is the opposite of action, strategy or trying – it cannot be accomplished, achieved or prescribed. Dr. Harry A. Tiebout, an early supporter of Alcoholics Anonymous, wrote:

> *With respect to…surrender, let me emphasize this point – it is an unconscious event, not willed by the patient even if he should desire to do so.*[1]

Again, it appears that there is no way out of the trap on its own terms. Yet, despite ego's reaction to this rather uncompromising claim, the fact that there is no hope is actually *not* bad news. How so? Because the fact that there never has been any hope for freedom at the level of individual (or egoic) choice or decision, along with the realization of this unalterable aspect of the universal human condition, finally exposes a simple truth: While you cannot do anything to secure your deliverance and the arrival of serenity, neither do you *need* do anything. What you can't do, in other words, you are *not required* to do. It is not far from the realization of this truth to the realization that we are actually *already at* our destination and have, in fact, always been there.

This truth initially strikes many of us as, at best, strange and, for some of us, as wrong and possibly even dangerous. It represents, moreover, a major offense to ego-based pride. Who or what are we humans if we do not, as individuals, possess free will, which has purportedly been given to each of us by God or perhaps by our neo-cortexes?

What is the basis for these incredible claims? Simply this: You cannot achieve what you already have. Or, more accurately, you cannot achieve what you already *are*. Again, what you are looking for – and wish to achieve – is none other than the one Self. The Self is what you seek. But the Self is also what is doing the seeking.

Here, in other words, is something we often miss in our frustration over not being able to lay hold of what we think we want: You cannot achieve or capture what you most want because what you most want is actually making the attempt to achieve or to capture! You are thus free of the compulsive effort to reach the goal of deep and abiding happiness because you have it already. Once again, more accurately, you *are* it.

Here is how Shankara put it:

A distinct and definite knowledge is possible in respect of everything capable of becoming an object of knowledge. But it is not possible in the case of That which cannot become an object. This is Brahma, the Knower. And the Knower can know other things, but cannot make Itself the object of Its own knowledge, in the same way that fire can burn other things but cannot burn itself. Neither can it be said that Brahma can be an object of knowledge for anything other than Itself, since outside Itself there is nothing which can possess knowledge.[2]

You can, in other words, grasp, objectify, achieve and name

everything *except* who it is you ultimately are – that which, in other words, is doing the grasping, objectifying, achieving and naming. For a human to frustrate himself, often for many years, with the futility of finding God or the Self only to realize, finally, that the efforts undertaken were of value *only to the extent that they revealed to the individual how ineffective and, indeed, how unnecessary they are,* represents an extraordinary and necessary phase of the transformation of conscious. To come to realize one's total impotence by way of actually trying to unify oneself with God is nothing less than the unlocking of the door to the kingdom of heaven, which forever remains locked until or unless one finds that both the door and its lock are illusions and that one need go nowhere and do nothing.

Anthony De Mello wrote:

Do I do anything to change myself?...You don't have to do anything. The more you do, the worse it gets. All you have to do is understand.[3]

Yet, we are, it seems, unable to see or to accept our freedom without first engaging in ego-based and willful attempts at getting what cannot, indeed, need not, be gotten. In this critical and ultimate sense, *everything* you've done or which has happened to you (or which has not happened to or for you) has, in fact, been entirely necessary. For it has brought you to readiness and openness as no other personal history could have.

To finally, by way of trying to attain enlightenment through purposeful efforts of the will, come to accept the futility of the enlightenment project is, as explained above, a critical phase of the awakening process. As long as any shred of hope remains that what one is seeking can be attained as you would attain a goal in the conventional sense, one is at risk of falling unconsciously into egoic, or personal, striving. Surrender thus must be deep. And any challenge that arises in one's life is ultimately for the purpose of undercutting and neutralizing the return of ego. Nothing convinces as does suffering of the unsustainability of the egoically-based enlightenment project – and the need to be free of it.

What then? What happens after what John Wheeler has called "the full stop"of egoic collapse?[4] Certainly the human body/mind organism known, in my case, as Karl, continues to exist. The radical displacement of ego from its former central position and the creation of what Carl Jung called "the new center" does not imply the immediate disappearance from the world of the human form despite the disappearance of the fictional and illusory person – now exposed as ego – who has been thought all along to be "contained" within this human form.

Here is the point at which sages past and present have invited us to simply notice (or watch, witness or observe) events both within and without. You are free, in other words, to be present to every thought, emotion or behavior which appears to arise from within and to forms of all types which appear in one's social and natural environment. For you are, in the ultimate sense, as so many teachers have pointed out for millennia, the witness to what appears and to what happens in the realm of form, time and space.

But, as the witness, you are "outside," so to speak, of the realm of form, time and space. You are thus the eternal, the formless within which all form arises and disappears. As Leo Hartong writes:

The Self is...watching...the grand show of the unfolding cosmic drama...the witness...is watching the show.[5]

Each of us *is* that witness and always have been. What's more, each of us possesses the unrestricted privilege of direct awareness and realization right here, right now. We need neither wait nor prepare ourselves any further.

So too, the fact that we are often in a state of unconsciousness is entirely irrelevant when we, again, wake up from it. As a client said to me recently, "It's so hard to maintain a sense of conscious connection to consciousness." I replied that she was making this statement from the standpoint of a "person" who feels she must achieve conscious connection. Her statement thus itself reflected false consciousness. But the state of false consciousness need not be attacked, repressed, fought against or resisted. There is no need to strain after, or push for, conscious connection. Instead, unconsciousness can be seen for what it is. Once seen, it fades away. You are ever the witness – of unconsciousness and everything else. Realization of this truth is all that matters ultimately.

---

[1] Tiebout, Harry "The Act of Surrender in the Therapeutic Process." Cited in Albers, Robert H. (1994); "Spirituality and Surrender: A Theological Analysis of Tiebout's Theory of Ministry to the Alcoholic" in *Journal of Ministry and Recovery*, Vol. 12 (2).

[2] Shankara, Adi "Commentary on Kena Upanishad." Cited in Watts, Alan (1972). *The Supreme Identity: An Essay on Oriental Metaphysic and the Christian Religion* (p. 48). Watts quoted this passage originally cited in Guenon (1945), *Man and His Becoming According to the Vedanta*, p. 114.

[3] De Mello, Anthony (1992). *Awareness: The Perils and Opportunities of Realty,* p. 90.

[4] Wheeler, John (2012). *Full Stop!: The Gateway to Present Perfection.*

[5] Hartong, Leo (2007). *Awakening to the Dream: The Gift of Lucid Living,* pp. 65-66.

✿

Chapter 6

Acute Desire Indicates that Self-Realization
is Happening

Viewed from the "big picture," therefore, efforts to grow spiritually can be understood as serving the critical purpose of revealing to us our powerlessness as persons. For we must become convinced of our utter inability, as egos, to realize the Self.

Yet, your desire for, and efforts to attain, spiritual growth, as futile as they are in actually reaching your goal, are also sure and certain indicators, as mentioned first in the "Introduction," that the process of deep connection with the spiritual center had already started before you even had the capacity to interpret your strivings as being essentially spiritual in nature. The Self, in other words, had begun, probably long ago, to stir in you uninvited by the conscious mind. You, to put it in slightly different terms, would not be reading these words if the Self (or God, the one, the center, the ground of being, Brahman or whatever you may wish to call it) had not already spontaneously initiated its awakening process by and through the human body/mind organism known, in my case, for example, as Karl.

Thus it is that the awakening of the Self that you are and always have been naturally issued in a conscious interest in spirituality. Indeed, your restlessness and discontent themselves continue to be signs that the spiritual experience is currently proceeding in you and by way of you. But know this, also: Your thirst is spiritual and so cannot be assuaged by any substitute for real spiritual water. What is this spiritual water? As alluded to several times already, the spiritual water for which you thirst is the Self, which is simply the experience of being aware. The ground of your being. That ground, moreover, has begun to "rise up," so to speak, in order to connect itself with itself at the conscious level. Again, if this phenomenon had not so begun, you would not be reading these words. It's as simple as that.

But the anxiety and emotional distress that generally accompanies the early phases of spiritual awakening is typically viewed as pathology by the world, including the mainstream mental health establishment. Indeed, the indicators of awakening are often reduced to symptoms of mental and emotional "disorders." Roberto Assiagioli put it as follows:

> ...*spiritual consciousness...before revealing itself in its positive form of enlightenment and expansion makes itself felt in a negative sense. When the process of psychospiritual transformation reaches its final and decisive stage, it sometimes produces intense suffering and an inner darkness which has been referred to by Christian mystics as the "dark night of the soul.*[1]

What's more, you've probably found little understanding among your family, friends and the community at large. Most of them don't, after all, consciously suffer from the overwhelming desire you have and so there is no way they can empathize.

Moreover, your feelings of being unique, eccentric, different or alienated from the mainstream might have begun as early as childhood. Maybe your inner experience and perceptions have been regularly categorized as mood, anxiety or personality disorders by the medical or mental health systems, which, despite highly notable exceptions, are based upon the assumption that emotional distress equals illness and that experts are required to alleviate your "condition." Perhaps you'd even begun to view yourself as "emotionally disturbed" and have believed that your "symptoms" arise from a past characterized by trauma, abuse, neglect and loss (all of which are certainly correlated with the distress you feel, but are not the ultimate causes of it).

"Oh God," said St. Augustine, "our hearts are restless until they find their rest in you." And, though Augustine's words state the truth for all persons, those who suffer from this aspect of the human condition – call it, perhaps, a sense of disconnection from the ground of being – at a chronic, or unconscious, level, tend to cling to mere substitutes for God. Thus the frantic drive for more of this, more of that covers over the Self's unconscious search for itself. For you, however, the Self's search for itself has become – or always was – not chronic but acute. You simply *must* know God and no substitute will suffice. "As a hart longs for flowing streams, so longs my soul for thee, O God," wrote the psalmist (Psalms 42:1). You could say the same.

Something, as we might put it, is, and has been, happening in, and by way of, you. "Something unknown," stated Sir Arthur Eddington, "is doing we don't know what." Refer to the experience in whatever terms you like. The process of transformation or enlightenment. Awakening. The rising up of the ground of being. Self-transcendence. God's will. Brahman seeking conscious connection with itself. The Tao. That which is. It doesn't really matter what you call it. Words, after all, only point; they contain no truth in and of themselves and are entirely relative.

The truth is that neither you nor I freely chose, as supposedly free agents or separate selves, to start out on the spiritual path. Those in whom the process has not begun – those, in other words, in whom the Self has not begun awakening – neither exhibit nor express interest in spiritual growth. This is not a problem or somehow inappropriate. Nor can currently uninterested persons be coaxed, from the "outside-in," to become spiritually engaged; the process must begin in them as it did in you – from the inside and work its way outward. If your encouragement has made a positive difference to the process of Self-discovery in another human, then it is because your "cheerleading," as we might call it, has connected with and encouraged a nascent or incipient process which, to some extent, was already alive in that person; your presence has provided an opportunity for a reinforcing synergy. This is a good and creative thing. But "you," conventionally understood as a person or ego, no more caused the process to begin in that human being than you caused it to begin in yourself.

In and by the concept of prevenient grace, Christian theology has professed an idea similar to this. Prevenient grace refers to grace given prior to human desire, action, decision or choice – even prior to human thought – and has been understood to be of the very nature of God's will. That Christian teaching and preaching has rarely been based upon a full understanding of the implications of prevenient grace is another matter and too far afield from our present considerations to pursue further here.

Instead, we must return to an examination of the experience

which is underway in you. By now, you might, in light of our discussion thus far, have concluded that what or who you take yourself to be – that to which you refer when you use the pronoun "I" or your name – is neither the origin of your search nor of the transformation you might have already noticed in yourself.

In short, through and by this or that particular human body/mind, the Self is seeking to move from the state of being half awake, which is of the essential nature of egoic, or human, consciousness and is the distinguishing feature which sets humans apart from the rest of nature, to full awakening. Eckhart Tolle believes that 10% or more of the population of North America are currently undergoing this transformation.[2]

But who is it that undergoes transformation? Who or what is the Self? And what is the difference between being partially awake (the state of human, egoic consciousness) and being fully awake? We must next take up these questions and others.

---

[1] Assagioli, Roberto (1991). *Transpersonal Development: The Dimension beyond Psychosynthesis*, pp. 112 and 127.

[2] Tolle has voiced this assessment at various times during his presentations.

✿

Chapter 7

How will You Know When What You Want Has Arrived?

The question which makes up the title of this chapter isn't actually as ridiculous as it sounds. After all, unless you are willing to call off the search when consciousness has found itself – that is, unless you remain uninvested in the search itself and can let it go once Self-realization has occurred – you can easily continue the search well beyond the point at which it has been apparently necessary. In other words, once you've been shown that the seeking phenomenon (or "the seeker") is *itself* what is being sought, you are free to stop seeking something which you have all along assumed that you lack. At that point, one can stop searching and start watching (or, as it is often put, witnessing).

Indeed, there is, you might agree, a significant difference between searching and witnessing. In the former you are looking for something which you believe you do not have. In the latter, you are simply noticing – or watching for when it doesn't seem to be present – something with which you have at least become somewhat familiar and perhaps have even come to know as the central aspect of who you are.

Thus it is that I often suggest to clients: "Watch for those times during which you are feeling at one with and connected to yourself." This is quite different from my saying "Keep searching," for instance, or "By the time you have returned for our next session, I will want you to have completed this task-based assignment." And I quite frequently add this assurance to my suggestion that the client simply notice or be aware: "If you watch for its appearance, you will notice it as soon as it arrives." Or: "If you watch for presence or peace, I promise you will see it." The "problem," indeed, has never been the actual absence of that for which we've been searching, but instead our strong human tendency to ignore or be unaware of it (consciousness having chosen to "lose itself" in form).

It is here, then. Right now. You, in fact, *are* it. No words, actions or thoughts need precede it as *it* precedes all thoughts, words and actions. Feel It. Enjoy It. And you'll never again be able to validly complain that you "don't have it."

❁

Chapter 8

Form and Formless

The term "witness," introduced in chapter 5, discussed further in chapter 7 and identified as who you ultimately are (as opposed to who you have always *assumed* that you are – that is, the illusory person existing, as most people seem to unconsciously believe, somewhere between the ears and behind the eyes), is roughly equivalent to the term "the formless" (though, as we will see, the formless refers to more than the witness). The formless, or witness, refers, in turn, to the "space" within which all form exists. The word "formless," moreover, is entirely synonymous with the infinite, the Self, Brahman, the Void, God, the Tao and pure consciousness.

The formless, then, is the eternal realm, the origin of all form (including space and time) and the "ground of being," to borrow a phrase from the 20th century theologian, Paul Tillich. Akin to Ken Wilber's spiritual realm, direct unmediated awareness – or pure subjective knowledge – of this dimension transforms consciousness. This is the dimension for which you have been, however unconsciously, seeking. William Law, the 18th century English theologian, described the relationship between the formless realm and the realm of the senses as follows: "Everything in temporal nature is descended out of that which is eternal."

The realm of form, on the other hand – akin to Wilber's rational and empirical realms – consists of anything or anybody that can be named or viewed as an object by the mind. Your thoughts, emotions, physical body and other physical bodies, ideas that go through your mind, other living beings and objects and things of all types are therefore forms.

The realm of form – roughly synonymous with what in spiritual parlance has often been called "the world" – need not be viewed as a problem requiring resolution. Neither need the world of form be escaped or resisted. The "problem" with the realm of form, or the world, lay in how the Self (in its state of mis-identification of itself as a human body/mind – a mis-identifcation that produces ego or the sense of separate selfhood) has viewed, or interpreted, the realm of form and what I, as ego, have expected from it. I (the pronoun "we" could be used here, of course, but ultimately each of us is "I" or the Self), however unconsciously, have been assuming all along that a new job, the next relationship, more money, a new place to live, having a child (or another one), attaining a leaner, fitter body, a new hobby or pastime or spiritual enlightenment (to suggest just a few examples of desire at work within the realm of form) will finally provide lasting happiness. Such is the illusion, compulsivity, and addictiveness – as has been discussed – of ego-centered human consciousness. Jesus refers to this phenomenon in the Gospel of St. Matthew, chapter 8: 26-27, wherein he uses the analogy of building one's house upon shifting and unstable sand to describe the foolishness of those who seek ultimate security in the realm of form.

It is important to note at this point, however, that the realms of form and formless are not opposites. All form has an opposite – the opposite of the human body/mind known as Karl, for example, is everyone and everything that is not Karl. The formless, on the other hand, has no opposite but transcends and includes all opposites within it. As written in the New Testament book, Acts of the Apostles: "In him we live and move and have our being" (Acts 17:28). There is nothing, in other words, that is not the formless (or God) at its "center," so to speak. John Scotus Erigena meant the same thing in his statement: "Every visible...creature is an... appearance of God."

Thus it is that the formless is *both* the space (or witness) within which all form exists *and* the animating "center" or will of all form. It has sometimes been said that what we see or otherwise experience by way of the senses, "hides" or "veils" God at the center of form. At other times, it is claimed that form is the expression of God at the center. Obviously both ways of putting it express truth.

The witness is, therefore, whether it consciously realizes it or not in this human form or that, witnessing itself! As Rupert Spira has written: "...the *content* of Consciousness *is* Consciousness itself. Consciousness is its own content. It never becomes anything else."[1] The formless, in other words, includes both the witness and what is witnessed.

This all-inclusive transcendence, moreover, is a phenomenon known in Sanskrit as "advaita," which, in English, is translated "non-dual" or "not two." We turn now to a discussion of this key and central feature of the Self, which you ultimately are, and which constitutes reality itself.

---

[1] Spira, Rupert (2008). *The Transparency of Things: Contemplating the Nature of Experience*, p. 51.

❖

Chapter 9

Non-Duality

It is important, I believe, to examine the phenomenon of non-duality with some degree of deliberateness. In so doing, we come to realize that "behind," so to speak, or "underneath" one's conscious awareness, along with all forms which one is, or may become, aware of, is the dimension of changeless and eternal awareness that is simultaneously both inaccessible (cannot ever be objectified, in other words) and your ultimate identity. We have called that dimension, among other terms that have been employed, the realm of the formless.

As noted above, the term "non-duality" means simply "not-two." One often encounters, in spiritual discourse, the term "oneness," which refers to the same phenomenon as does non-duality. But the word and concept, "oneness," in that it can easily imply an opposite, such as "multiplicity," has quite frequently been avoided by spiritual teachers through the ages in favor of non-duality, as the latter term less equivocally designates a key feature of the formless dimension: the formless, again, has no opposite.

The non-dual nature of the formless realm upon which, as we have discussed, the realm of form is based or grounded, implies that all opposites which the human mind overlays, or superimposes, onto the flux-and-flow of reality – up/down, light/darkness, good/evil, right/left, male/female, myself/other (Wilber calls this last pair "the primary dualism" as it is the first to appear in humans and so, generally speaking, is the last to disappear in the process of transformation), even form/formless – are ultimately not opposed to, or separate from, each other, as they appear to be. Instead, they are underlain by, or infused with, the formless from which they emanate. And, it is worth repeating, the formless is both the aware witness to each pole of all opposites and, simultaneously, that which "is doing," or animating, each pole. To put it another way, the one witness of all action is watching itself as the one actor of all parts in the universal drama, or play (*maya* in the original Sanskrit). Actor and audience are one and the same. There is, once again to cite Wilber, "no boundaries" anywhere in the universe.[1] Or, if you prefer, the stage upon which the play or drama is being acted and the players are ultimately the same.

Wayne Liquorman writes:

Everything is the functioning of Consciousness, because Consciousness is all there is...Everything is Consciousness... Everything that happens is Consciousness...Consciousness is the source and substance of everything.[2]

Consciousness is, then, we could say, the only reality as it is the ground or essence of all form as well as the space within which all form exists. Consciousness is thus the irreducible phenomenon without which nothing could exist. Before the Big Bang event of 14.7 billion years ago, which resulted in the appearance of the world of form, there was only formless consciousness. Consciousness, moreover, has no past or future and is entirely outside of time and space while, at the same time, provides the basis for everything within time and space. Only consciousness, which, again, is essentially non-dual, is real.

Coventry Patmore meant the same thing in her statement: "Only the divine is real."

---

[1]   Wilber, Ken (1981). *No Boundary: Eastern and Western Approaches to Personal Growth.*

[2]   Liquorman, Wayne (2004). *Never Mind: A Journey into Non-Duality,* p. 28.

✧

Chapter 10

The Formless Awakening in Form

Thus it is that the non-dual and inaccessible – though entirely present – formless dimension (which underlies, or precedes, every form, including the opposite concepts "form" and "formless") freely chose, in the aforementioned event known as the Big Bang, to identify itself with form while continuing, simultaneously, to provide the space within which all form exists and acts. This "kenosis," biblical Greek for "self-emptying," is described in the New Testament book of Philippians (2:5-7) in the following passage:

Have this mind among yourselves, which is yours in
Christ Jesus, who, though he was in the form of God,
did not count equality with God a thing to be grasped,
*but **emptied himself**...being born in the likeness of men.*
[emphasis mine]

In so freely abandoning itself to form, the Self created what appears to be multiplicity, separation and, in the case of humans, individual wills.

Yet, the Self's unconscious identification with form, however many billions of years it has lasted and will continue to last and however necessary it is for the play or drama of life as we know it to go on, is not the omega, or end point, of the Self's journey. Specifically through the human species, the Self is clearly seeking an awakening to itself and wills to express itself consciously in finite (or form) terms. The Self's finding of, or realizing of, itself, after having chosen to lose itself in form, is the birth, by and through particular humans, of "(ego) self-transcendence."

Here, then, is a dis-identification of the Self from its identification with ego, or personal, form. Ego, or conventional human, consciousness is thus the necessary, partially awakened, transitional phase or bridge between totally unconscious identification with form – that is, the world of non-human nature or, using Wilber's terms, "pre-egoic" consciousness – and "trans-egoic" consciousness, in which the Self has "re-connected" with itself. "I" apparently, before it realizes its true identity as the Self, first awakens from full unconsciousness and identifies itself with individual human body/mind organisms while, at the same time, dis-identifying itself with everything and everyone which is *not* this or that particular human body/mind.

The strong momentum which drives the egoic consciousness which results from the Self's identification with human body/minds, however, is eventually exhausted and thus makes room for the Self in full and purely subjective realization of itself, the omega point of the Self's journey back to itself.

Alan Watts wrote:

> *Realization is the Self emerging from its own voluntary "slumber" of complete identification with a finite point of view, and it occurs at the moment when one finds oneself able to will and consciously accept the precise point at which one stands....For this constitutes a consciousness of perfect harmony between one's own will and the divine*

will and the further discovery that the two are one. The ego as such can never make this discovery because it can no more accept itself...than a musical instrument can play itself. However, the very fact that man, as an ego, can attempt to accept or to know himself is the certain sign that he is more than ego and is beginning to realize it.[1]

---

[1] Watts, Alan (1972). *The Supreme Identity: An Essay on Oriental Metaphysic and the Christian Religion*, pp. 182-183.

❁

Chapter 11

Consciousness Becoming Fully Aware of Itself

For many of us, this point at which the Self begins dis-identi-fying from ego, is perplexing. We begin asking, "What is aware of what? If I feel myself more and more to be the awareness underlying all form rather than any one specific form, then what does it mean to say that 'I am aware of myself?' Is there one of me or two?" Who are you? Are you the conscious mind? Or something that "inhabits" this body of yours? And is it to the mind, the body or the "inhabitant" of the body that we refer when we use the pronoun "I" or our names? Or is conscious thinking – along with feeling and acting – simply activities within a universal whole and the thinker, feeler and actor (or ego self, or soul, supposedly "centered" in the body) which presumably actually does the think-ing, acting and feeling only an unexamined assumption, illusion or conditioned reaction pattern that somehow goes along with the human condition?

Let's assume that you are at least willing to consider that you are much more than you've believed yourself to be. That you have come to believe that the story, which began on a specific date of birth, of a supposed individual person, who has had a unique history of experiences and who will someday die, might be so limited that it has become necessary to look deeper. If so, you may be willing to define who you are as transcending the apparently person-containing organism which you have all along taken to be your identity.

In fact, you might have even experienced flashes of insight during which you have come to realize that the word "self" is actually synonymous with the words "the whole" or "the entire universe" rather than with the supposed person.

Eastern religions, along with certain mystical and esoteric interpretations of western religion – however much they fall short, as do all religions in their popular forms, in representing ultimate truth – have been quite explicit in defining the Self that you are as being identical to Brahman, the Tao or universal mind and that the truth of your identity as the one Self must be realized not through speculative philosophy, reason or doctrine, but through personal experience. So too, since the Self cannot know itself objectively (as there is no subject/object separation in the Self), to know who you are by way of thinking, analysis or reasoning is impossible. Moreover, the apparent boundary between oneself and everyone and everything else is thus entirely illusory.

Alan Watts, for one, was fond of asking: "Who or what is it, after all, that beats your heart, grows your hair and regulates your glands – all without conscious attention or effort?" This all happens automatically, you might say. Another word for "automatically" could be, of course, "involuntarily." In other words, these things happen of themselves.

But there are other things – tying your shoe, getting out of bed, turning on your computer, picking up this book, preparing your lunch, making a telephone call, facilitating a meeting – which happen voluntarily. And voluntary actions and involuntary events, though opposites, go together, as we have discussed above, in the same way that two sides of the same coin go together. You can't have one without the other. There thus must be a unifying principle, or one undivided, universal thinker, feeler and actor which transcends the opposites, includes both, holds them together and is the hidden source of all events, including all thoughts, emotions and actions, both voluntary and involuntary.

As first discussed in Chapter 2, this underlying, or transcendent, dimension is what the ancient Chinese philosophers referred to as the Tao, or the way or course of nature. This is, also, what Hindus have referred to as Brahman, the source of all form and also the universal actor at the heart of all form who simultaneously plays all the parts in the drama of life at this level of existence. Buddhists have called the transcendent dimension the Void, claiming that it is the emptiness out of which all events emanate. Jung called it the Self. Mystics have sometimes referred to it with the term God.

This dimension, then, whatever you choose to call it, is, as also discussed above, becoming aware of itself by and through the body/mind known conventionally as John, Mary, Dick, Susan or whatever your name happens to be. Thus it is that you, like me, are ultimately that one Self.

In other words, the Self in the role of "I, Karl Galten," for example, had been enthralled for many years by its apparent identity as a separate, individual person (or ego) with a unique history and a name. Now, though, it has "awakened from the dream" (to borrow a very descriptive phrase from Leo Hartong[1]) of separation and has realized its true identity as that still and pure dimension which has been witnessing (or "containing") the human body/mind organism known as Karl Galten, as well as playing the part of, Karl Galten. At the very same time, the Self has been containing, and playing the part of, every other form in the entire universe, as well, and has been doing so for billions of years. I am thus just as much the social and natural environment within which Karl Galten exists as I am the body/mind known as Karl Galten.

So what of the person, or ego, which was assumed to be the entity named Karl, who was thought to have been born on a specific date and which had appeared to correspond to the pronoun "I"? It turns out that this individual, or apparently separate, self was always only a very convincing illusion created by the Self's mis-identification, as noted above, with this particular human body/ mind. "I," in fact, refers not to a guy (or "soul") inside a body who exercises a will apart from the whole of the universe. Instead "I" refers to the Self and does so wherever the pronoun "I" is spoken, however relatively few still are the points at which "I" is spoken in full consciousness of its supreme identity.

The thirst for spiritual experience – both in its cruder varieties and in its more evolved patterns – was always based upon, and driven by, a deeply unconscious, unquestioned and ultimately false assumption that I am a separate person. Instead, I am the universal, timeless, formless and spaceless consciousness. As John Greven has written:

> *All human suffering is due to a case of mistaken*
> *identity – a core belief in a conceptual separate self. This*
> *appears as an unexamined assumption that there is a*
> *"me," a self-center that exists as a separate entity. On*
> *investigation this "me" is found to be a phantom. On*

looking into our actual experience there is a seeing into
the illusory nature of this self we call "I" or "me." Then
the realization dawns that this apparent "me" is nothing
more substantial than a thought appearing in the open
space of pure Presence/Awareness.[2]

And so , I would propose to the reader that the question asked
above, "Who is aware of what?" is ultimately answerable, to the
extent that words and ideas can be helpful, as follows: "I, as universal consciousness (or the Self or witness), have realized, in full
subjectivity, myself as universal consciousness." The division, then,
between I and not-I, which is the primary and fundamental division that the Self still needs to overcome while identified with the
human, has been transcended. I have come together with myself
at last. And I am at peace.

---

[1] From the book by that title, cited above in Chapter 5.

[2] Greven, John (2005). *Oneness: The Destination You Never Left*,
    p. 88.

✿

Chapter 12

Your True Identity

"An invisible and subtle essence is the Spirit of the whole universe. That is reality. That is truth. You are That" says the "Chandog ya Upanishad." "Tat tvam asi," Sanskrit for "You are that," has been called the central thesis of Advaita Vedanta, and is equivalent to Jesus' saying in the Gospel of John (10:30), "I and the Father are One," as both sayings identify the deepest aspect of form, including the human form, to be the essential basis, or ground, of the entire universe.

Now if you are it, you obviously have no ultimate need for anything as everything is contained within the totality of the Self, now understood not as the individual and personal ego self (or *jivatman* in Sanskrit) – that supposed entity with a name and a history, that "mind-made" self, as Eckhart Tolle calls it, and what heretofore you had assumed was the entity being referred to when you use the pronoun "I" – but as the ultimate center out of which time, space and all form proceeds. Richard Sylvester writes:

> *Liberation is freedom from the burden of being a person....What a wonderful relief it is to see that there is no choice, no person, no separation. Nothing you have ever done has ever led to anything because you have never done anything. No one has ever done anything although it appears that things have been done...Isn't it*

wonderful that you have never made a choice in your life? There is nothing to regret, nothing to feel guilty about. Nothing could ever have been any different, nothing could ever have been any other way. Isn't that a relief?...You can let it all go, you can release all the tension.[1]

There is thus no basis upon which one can posit even the existence of a separate self or will, a supposed entity which ultimately must be placed into the category of illusion or fiction, however overwhelmingly convincing the illusion has been and remains for the majority of humans at present.

Certainly Jesus realized his ultimate and true identity as evidenced by his statement, "He who has seen me has seen the Father" (John 14: 9). It is also the conclusion that we are likely to draw as a result of the experience of spiritual transformation. For the arrival of new consciousness brings with it profound implications for our very sense of who we are. In fact, what we call "awakening" is simply the realization that your ultimate identity, as stated above, is BOTH the witness to all form AND, simultaneously, the center, or ground, of each form that exists. There is thus no "other."

---

[1]   Sylvester, Richard (2005). *I Hope You Die Soon: Words on Non-Duality*, p. 23.

❀

Chapter 13

More on Ego

In spiritual circles the word "ego" is used quite frequently and the present writing is obviously no exception. Yet, so often this word, basic and fundamental as it is to spiritual teaching, is itself misunderstood.

Though it would seem evident, for instance, that there are as many egos as there are normally developed human beings over the age of about 18 months, ego, being in the form of a pattern of mis-identification on the part of the one Self, is, as an aspect of the Self, actually indivisible.

Here is the point that many of us understand, and even use, the word "ego" in ways that tend to perpetuate illusion. Under the pervasive influence of psychoanalytic thought (which has always employed the word "ego" to correspond to the conscious "part" of the human person), we tend to regard ego as something I "have." We say, for example, "My ego is too large," or "I want my ego to die." What we do not realize is that I, as I conventionally understand myself, *am* ego. In other words, spiritually (not psychoanalytically) speaking, ego refers to the illusion of separate selfhood or individuality which the Self is actually, in the time and place known, for example, as "Karl," believing itself to be.

Recall, for a moment, that humans are a relatively late arrival on planet earth. Following the Big Bang, which scientists tell us occurred some 14.7 billion years ago and which constituted the primal Self "blowing itself out" into a freely willed alienation from itself, the Self existed as millions of pre-human forms. Rock, fire, water – the latter of which made plant life possible and from out of which eventually came creatures, who, through billions of years of evolution, came to live on land – amphibians, reptiles, early mammals and the like. The Self remained, as these creatures and plant life, completely and unconsciously identified with the realm of form and, as those millions of non-human species which still exist, the Self remains fully "lost" in, or identified with, form. My cat, for instance, in that his field of consciousness is unbroken by a sense of individuality or "I-ness," cannot conceive of the dualism "myself" versus "other." He is thus an example of "pre-egoic" consciousness.

By way of the human, though, the Self, previously in deep and unselfconscious "sleep" in the realm of form (while, recall, at the same time, remaining the omnipresent witness of all form – the Self witnessing itself), has partially awakened. Indeed, in the human, awareness of "I" has come about.

And yet, human (or ego) consciousness is nonetheless still fundamentally based upon illusion in that, as the human, the Self has evolved from a full identification with form to having dis-identified from everything except individual human body/minds which, one could say, is an identification, upon the dawning of Self-consciousness, with the most proximate form. Self-consciousness (or "I-ness"), in other words, has arrived, but is assumed by the Self to correlate with human organisms.

This dis-identification from what now is viewed as "other" represents a step "up and out" of pre-egoic consciousness. Indeed, ego consciousness, created by the Self's mis-identification of itself and which, for millennia, has been of the essence of socially conditioned misunderstandings of to whom and to what the pronoun "I" refers, has been the defining feature of the human species. The capacity to actually use the pronoun "I," in other words, both distinguishes humans from other life forms and, at the same time, introduces into the Self's universal play of maya (or "illusion") a certain instability in that "I" now actually sense, however vaguely, an aloneness and an alienation from my true Self.

Moreover, because the Self's own will has, since the aforementioned Big Bang event, been an eventual re-unification with itself, human ego consciousness represents not an endpoint in spiritual evolution, but a bridge between the Self in full identification with form and the Self in full and complete subjective realization of itself (its state prior to the Big Bang).

As thus a transition between the "pre-egoic" (full identification with form) and the "trans-egoic" (or full union of the Self with itself), egoic consciousness, sensing its apparent separation from its true home as no pre-egoic life form can or does, is particularly prone to anxiety, having left the non-problematic security of pre-egoic and unconscious union with itself, to which it cannot return. Jesus' "Parable of the Prodigal Son," told in the gospel of St. Luke, chapter 15, probably the most well-known and loved of the New Testament parables, describes, by way of metaphor, the primal pre-egoic state, the subsequent state of separation and suffering (egoic) and the return of consciousness to identification with and as the Self (trans-egoic consciousness).

Today this "return home," as noted in Chapter 6, has been estimated as occurring in approximately 10% of humans. Among that significant minority, there are, of course, gradations from early phases of awakening to full union. And, while the claim that the Self is currently awakening to its true identity in around 10% of us may not be a dramatic one, this percentage is much higher than was the case only a mere 50 years ago.

Thus it is that ego, being, again, the creation of the Self's identification with human body/minds, is not what "wakes up" to its true identity. Instead, it is the Self which, at the time and place known conventionally as "Karl," awakens and realizes that it has been playing a role and has forgotten that "Karl" is but a surface appearance, a mask and thus a false identity. The Self is therefore free, as it awakens from its dream of not only "playing Karl" but actually *being* Karl, to dis-identify from the role and to simultaneously identify with itself. The role of Karl need not be abandoned and can still be played while it exists in the world. But the role can now be played *consciously* – that is, played by awareness, now aware of itself, and no longer in thrall to, or hypnotized by, form identity.

There is thus no need to fight ego or to try getting rid of it. In fact, the act of resisting ego is predicated upon an assumption that "I," as an individual, must be rid of "my ego." This assumption is itself egoic. As Lao Tsu, author of the Tao Te Ching, said, "Trying to get rid of ego is a positive manifestation of ego." We are free, instead, to simply be aware of ego from the position of the one witness, a practice which clearly and convincingly verifies for you that – since it is impossible for you to see and to objectively know your true Self – you are not ego.

Moreover, if you're not ego, you must be the witness of ego and, analogously, of all form. As awareness, I am the irreducible and necessary "space," synonymous with the term "witness," within which all form exists. However, as the Isha Upanishad puts it:

In the heart of all things, of whatever there is in the universe, dwells the Lord. He alone is the reality.

So, while the witness, I am also at the heart of everything that is witnessed, or, in other words, form of all types. The witness is thus, despite the infinite variety and array of outward appearances which physical, emotional, behavioral and cognitive form takes, at all times and places witnessing none other than its own very Self.

You are that Self.[1]

---

[1] It might seem contradictory to claim, on the one hand, that the Self must dis-identify from all form, including the human, on its way toward full Self-realization, and, on the other hand, to maintain that the Self remains "in the heart of all things." But this is in keeping with the Self's non-dual nature in that, while the Self must ultimately *identify* as the witness to form and not with form itself, the Self remains the ground of all form. As long as form exists, in other words, it is entirely contingent upon the will of the Self. Again, the central issue is that of identity, not existence. The Self is always witnessing nothing other than itself.

Chapter 14:

Can Your True Identity as the Self be Verified?

Do you need further convincing that you are the constantly awake consciousness within which all form exists and, at the same time, the living center of all form? Then look and see. Simply be conscious of being conscious. It is absolutely undeniable that consciousness is present. If it were not, you would not exist and couldn't even be reading these words. In fact, consciousness is, as implied in the previous chapters, the eternal and unchanging dimension of you. Obviously words cannot capture this truth. But consciousness – which is the same phenomenon as has been called by many teachers the eternal now – is what's "really real" about you. All else is changing form and thus, though existent, is not fully real.[1]

Recall at this point that the essential definition of enlightenment is consciousness conscious of itself. Thus it is that noticing (or being aware of, witnessing or observing) consciousness, which, in the untransformed human condition we ignore or are unaware of, is the omega point of human existence, the very purpose of the human species and the shift at which egoic consciousness becomes trans-egoic consciousness – that is, in a moment-by-moment state of realization of its ultimate identity.

But no, becoming conscious of consciousness is not something that you, as John, Dick or Mary *need* to do. There is, after all, no need to get to a place at which you are already. Neither is becoming conscious of consciousness a prescription, law, imperative or method. Indeed, enlightenment is not an ego project. Instead, being conscious of consciousness (or "Self-aware") is your birthright. In short, you need do nothing. Yet, you are free at all times and in all circumstances to be conscious of consciousness itself. This is of the essence of simplicity.

"How incredible each moment is." writes Jeff Foster. "How undeniable...This takes no effort. No knowledge. This is not something to be attained. This is utter obvious presence....this is the liberation that is sought."[2]

---

[1] For an excellent discussion of the varying levels of reality, see Deutsch, Elliot (1973). *Advaita Vedanta.*

[2] Foster, Jeff (2007). *Beyond Awakening: The End of the Spiritual Search*, p. 112.

✻

Chapter 15

The Seeker is Thus the Sought

The seeker is seeking, however unconsciously, for itself. We perhaps are ready for a deeper exploration of this truth, which was first described in chapter one.

Let us, therefore, ask ourselves these questions: In addition to the realization of your ultimate identity (or Self-realization), are there further implications for us of the non-dual nature of reality? Of "Tat tvam asi" ("You are that") for the spiritual search itself? Of consciousness becoming conscious of itself in the time and place known conventionally as John, Dick or Mary?

By now it might be clear to the reader that, in your craving for "something more" in this world or in your inner world, you have been manifesting nothing less than the Self's search for itself. In other words, as noted earlier, you have been looking for the most real, but overlooked, aspect of yourself.

No – the point needs repetition – this is not Karl looking for Karl. Karl's very existence has always, after all, been predicated upon a mind-made, thus entirely illusory, self which supposedly has his own personal history, date of birth, goes by the name "Karl" and resides in the head. As has been stated several times from slightly differing perspectives above, the ego, or separate self, is nothing more than the result of the Self's mis-identification with a human body/mind and disappears upon the Self's coming to know itself in the eternal now's pure subjectivity, in which there is no further perceived need for a separate self.

But, as has also been claimed above, the searcher will never come to know itself as an object which can be named, analyzed, talked or thought about or in any sense grasped by reason or the senses. When you realize this, you will also notice the diminishment and eventual stoppage of the restless search. If you, indeed, are all there is, there is no need to find anything or anyone. Once again, "Tat tvam asi" – "You are that." There is ultimately no "other."

Occasionally I have noticed that sudden realization of true identity is not necessarily pleasing to some people. "Then what is there to do?" one apparent ego self might say. "What's the point then?" others say. Radical relativity and the sudden disappearance of compulsion can be too much, at times, and the Self might retreat, however temporarily, to earlier phases of consciousness so as to preserve the compelling belief in separateness that seems, to many people, so critical to a sense of meaning and purpose.

For others, though – those in whom the Self is truly ready – Self-realization comes as a welcome release from the trap which had seemed so intractable. For these seekers, many of whom have suffered long and intensely, the ultimately dysfunctional nature of ego had become so acute and unmanageable that identification as the Self and dis-identification from the old and illusory egoic identity is by far the most meaningful and profound experience of their entire lives.

Most often, of course, awakening, even if the Self doesn't initially retreat from it, is followed by what Eckhart Tolle calls a transitional phase, in which ego identity and identification as the

Self alternates, sometimes for many years. To some, this transition is frustrating, as if the ego illusion, if it would only "buckle down," could make the transition to full and abiding Self-awareness more quickly. But, of course, an illusion is, by definition, not capable of doing anything and to desire a quicker transition is, at any rate, egoic and, therefore, unnecessary. The Self in any place and time awakens at the rate to which it freely chooses.

Indeed, many of us eventually come to see the apparently slow progress the Self seems to be making as only another mind-made "problem" rooted, as it is, in the assumption that the passage of linear and conventional time, itself a construct and not real, is the key element in the Self's awakening.

But the passage of time is unrelated to the Self's awakening as the Self awakens now, and now, in its eternal nature, is outside time and space. Thus it is that the Self, as it seems to go back-and-forth between consciousness and unconsciousness of itself, is really alternating between identification with the mind-made and illusory personal self, which corresponds with the realm of time, form and space and, in full subjectivity, with itself, which corresponds to the eternal, the infinite and the formless. Further, at the very millisecond of re-awakening, the fact that the Self may have been, just seconds before, at the end of a prolonged state of sleep and identification with the human form is of no relevance whatsoever. For there is no past and one is again free. As Tim Freke has written:

> *And then, unexpectedly and inexplicably, it happens. My train of thought jolts to a halt.....I'm overwhelmed by awesome, unfathomable, breathtaking mystery...I seem to have inexplicably slipped into another reality...I'm immersed in wonder. I feel a bizarre sense of oneness*

with everything.....as if I'm the universe looking at itself...
The humdrum world has peeled away like a superficial
veneer, revealing a secret garden that I've always
suspected was close by. I know this place. It feels like
home.[1]

What's more, no precautions need be taken to avoid falling again under the spell of time, space and form as such effort would only represent ego's attempts at making itself indispensable and at the center of an awakening project. But there is no project and there is no need for one. The Self awakens entirely on its own, by itself and apart from egoic effort. It also chooses where and when to awaken. And it is always right on schedule. We can know and trust that.

---

[1] Freke, Tim (2009). *How Long is Now: A Journey to Enlightenment...*
and Beyond, p. 14.

❋

Chapter 16

Making Spiritual Progress

Yet, many, probably most, of us become concerned now and then with whether or not we (or, more precisely, the Self who is each of us) are reaching the end of the transitional stage quickly enough. This is entirely understandable given the nature of our deeply conditioned, unconscious and (up-till-now) unquestioned assumption that we are individuals who must, if we are to get anywhere in life, exert conscious, purposeful and willful effort toward the accomplishment of goals.

But "Who is there to make progress?" asks John Greven.

All of this is happening within the presence/awareness that you are. The One, that you are, is already whole and complete and there is nothing to gain. What you are is in perfect working order with no improvement needed or possible. Is there anything wrong with your beingness?[1]

"Ah," says the mind, "so really what you're saying is that all is determined by fate, God or destiny and that I am essentially a puppet on a string. Puppets don't need to choose improvement or work to become more enlightened. All is being done for them."

But the mind's complaint – and it is a common one – is still based upon the demonstrably false assumption that there is an "I" that can be determined, fated or dangled from a puppeteer's string and, over time, arrive at whatever destination has been planned for her.

But – to repeat – you are not a "little self" who inhabits a body, which goes by a name, was born and will die some day. There is no such entity, not in the body through which this book has been written and not in the body through which reading it is taking place. There is "no one home here," so to speak, and no one home there, either. What you and I are is the space of awareness within which all forms – including these body/minds – appear to act independently. We are also, at the same time, the center, as we have called it, of each form which, at least in the human, makes it possible to say "I" – that is, to have Self-consciousness. But that center is not a willing, independent ego self apart from the whole. That center is instead an aspect of the larger field of awareness within which it acts, thinks and feels. As noted earlier, witness and what is witnessed are one and the same. And the pronoun "I" refers to the one Self at all times.

Extraordinary? Yes it is. Moreover, knowledge of the seamless, non-dual wholeness of the universe is enlightenment. Once you've realized this truth, you will feel a freedom to go forward in joy and abandonment.

Even that compelling question of spiritual progress loses its dramatic seriousness when one realizes that nothing and no one could be right now any way other than the way it/he/she is. That, of course, includes the gradation at which you assess yourself to be on the transition from old consciousness to new. As Ram Dass has said, "Don't you see that everything is already perfect?!"

---

[1] Greven, John (2005). *Oneness: The Destination You Never Left*, p. 67.

✿

Chapter 17

But I Still Don't Feel It

If I had a dollar for every time I have heard this complaint – "But I don't feel that perfect oneness"– from a client with whom I have been discussing freedom, alas, I'd probably be wealthy today. So let's look at this concern.

Generally speaking, complaints that we don't feel – or understand – spiritual truth are sure indicators that we're expecting something from a teaching that we believe we haven't yet gotten. Something in our experience still feels missing no matter how many books we read, retreats or talks we attend or how often we may sit in meditation. "There must be something more," we reason, "since I'm still feeling empty, restless and discontent. What's wrong?"

I find the words of Jeff Foster instructive here, as he has described our attempts to attain "more" spirituality:

It is the wanting itself which destroys the possibility of ever having what you want, for the wanting implies that something can be captured and owned by someone. But who could ever capture, and who could ever own?

There is only this, and this can never be captured, because it is not a thing amongst other things, but the open, spacious possibility of possibilities which gives rise to all things in the first place.

*What we really want is an end to our wanting, but
even the wanting of an end to wanting is another want,
perhaps the biggest want of them all.*

*Wanting implies that there is something to get: but is
there really anything to get in the first place, or was
our wanting always only in vain? Perhaps the wanting
obscures the obvious: we already have everything we
could ever want, because right now, an end to all our
wants, all our desires, all our problems is already with us,
and that end is so simple: these desires, problems, wants,
troubles, annoyances do not really exist, in that they are
simply thoughts arising now. That's all they are, all the
troubles of the world: thoughts.*

*And so really, what we want is an end to thought. But
wouldn't that just be more thinking?*

*But an end to thought is not really needed. Thought
happens, thought appears, and there is nobody doing it.*[1]

In other words, as we first considered in Chapter 3, acting
purposefully with the end in mind of increasing one's spiritual
state is to find oneself back in the self-perpetuating cycle. But to
purposefully *avoid* the attempt to increase one's spiritual state is,
likewise, to only trigger the same vicious cycle! There is thus, to
re-visit a point made earlier, no escape from this conundrum on
its own terms and many of us eventually "hit bottom" here, having come to the undeniable conclusion that there is really nothing
we can do. We may have previously given mere lip service to this
truth; but now we're feeling it all the way down into our depths.

Twelve Step programs refer to this phenomenon as "powerlessness." In the early Middle Ages, St. Augustine wrote of it and, in the 16th century Martin Luther referred to it as the "bondage of the will." And, if you too have become aware of the compulsivity of the human condition at work in you, you are fortunate indeed.

So now that we have once again come up against this pernicious issue, what are we to do? But, as always, this is the wrong, if entirely understandable, question.

To return to an earlier metaphor, a non-swimmer thrown overboard significantly increases his chances of drowning by struggling for security and safety. In this same sense, we ensnare and entangle ourselves further by striving to attain enlightenment. The experiential fact is that anything we do with the purpose in mind of attaining what we believe to be "more" or "better" spirituality only makes our predicament worse.

"So," you say, "how do I stop trying?" By now, the reader has very probably begun to see the infinitely regressive nature of the problem. As first discussed in Chapter 4, if trying is the problem, then trying not to try is equally the problem. Some of us have come to the point of near despair over this dilemma.

So what's the answer? Now this is a potentially better question, and it was first addressed in Chapter 5. This question at least doesn't imply purposeful and egoic effort, agency or goal-directedness. The answer, one might suggest, is that there is no answer. If I am unable to attain enlightenment, if achieving it is truly not an ego project, then I may as well acknowledge my powerlessness as an individual. This could be "bad news," at least from ego's perspective.

But where bad news is identified, good news is never far away. For powerlessness is itself a two-sided coin. One side of the coin says "You can't get enlightenment." The other side says "Neither are you required to get it." But then, how do I get it? Do you see the hopelessness of this?

What's more, there is another quirky thing about our confused human predicament: Although we can sometimes, often after a considerable ordeal, admit that we have no power to change a person or situation, to then take the next step and say "But neither do I need to try" is something else again and seems to fly in the face of our very sense of guilt-driven initiative. To take that step represents a new level of humility, realization of one's true identity as the Self, and, ultimately, a profound sense of gratitude and consummate peace. Fact is, to once again emphasize this point, what we have never lost doesn't need to be regained.

In the meantime, what of our distress and suffering? "We are healed of suffering only by experiencing it to the full" said Marcel Proust. In other words, just feel it. Go with it. Permit it to pour over and through you. It is thus discharging itself from the body/mind while, at the very same time, purging consciousness of ego. What we have always struggled against, pushed down, resisted, tried to get rid of or reason away – ego and our pain – can simply and finally be allowed to happen. Oh what a relief. And what a lifting of the dense and dark cloud made up of ego and accumulated suffering.

---

[1] Foster, Jeff (2007). *Beyond Awakening: The End of the Spiritual Search*, p. 71.

❁

Chapter 18

Envisioning Yourself at Peace

"When you've received what you've come here for, how will things be different?" I frequently ask counseling clients this question. It tends to engage the imagination and put it to use in actually creating the conditions for which the client seeks. But, as always, envisioning oneself at peace is no mandate, method, technique or imperative; you are free to do this, but don't "have to" as if doing so is tied – or should be tied – to a specific outcome.

Given your choice of reading this book, you are qualified, as we have discussed earlier, to be called a "spiritual seeker." As a spiritual seeker, I will ask you a similar question to the one above: "When you have become sufficiently enlightened, what will be different in your life?"

I have heard a number of good responses to this question, including "My relations with others will be more harmonious." "I'll handle things with ease rather than with anxiety or compulsivity," "I'll be more confident" and "I'll experience depth-level joy and serenity."

You might consider your own response(s) to this question. At one time, my own answers to this question would have included: "I will be at peace with myself," "I will be happy rather than always depressed and anxious," "I'll finally find a life partner," "I'll obtain meaningful work" and "I will break free of this constant and nagging sense of dread, guilt and doom."

My responses today to someone who'd articulated the above hopes would be among the following: "So why not live in the peace that you already feel, however small you feel that peace is at present?" "Go ahead and feel whatever happiness there is in you." "You are free to do your work while paying special attention to whatever meaning there is in it." "Live as if there is no cloud of dread hanging over you (even if you believe there actually is such a cloud hanging over you)."

Your hopes might be similar to what mine were or be quite different in significant ways. And yet, whatever they are, let me say this to you: "You are free now – with no further preparation or cleansing away of guilt necessary – to go ahead and live in these new ways."

So too, in all of these things, know that the consciousness that you deeply and fundamentally are is expanding and growing and that you are becoming more familiar with it. This process will neither stop nor be permanently reversed.

The consciousness that you are has chosen to awaken in and by this human. Could anything come close to being more important for you than this? "The highest to which man can attain is wonder," said Johann Goethe. To become more and more aware in the present moment of your true identity as underlying and changeless consciousness is to live in wonder – and you will agree with me that nothing the mind could produce or the world could give comes even close to this.

✾

Chapter 19

Suffering

When I look back upon my life, I recall many years of suffering. My unhappiness had begun in childhood and had expanded during adolescence. By the age of 17, I was an alcoholic.

The beginning of recovery from alcoholism in my 20's improved my functioning, but my unhappiness remained in the form of generalized, and almost continuous, anxiety.

About two years into recovery, I began experiencing panic episodes which lasted the better part of another two years, a period which I look back upon now as a positive turning point in my recovery and in my life, in general.

Yet, integration of mind, body and spirit proceeded gradually and the emotional distress which had been generated from deep within since childhood decreased, I believe now, precisely at the rate at which the lessons that the suffering was designed to bring me were integrated into consciousness.

Here, then, is the very purpose of suffering: To promote spiritual awakening. And those of us – which probably includes readers of this book – who have suffered most acutely are usually the most ready for awakening.

In my counseling practice, it is a rare day when a client doesn't ask a question such as: "Why do I feel the way I do? Where does this come from?," "Why can't I be happy?" or "Why can't I be like other people?"

These are questions that I regularly asked myself and others for many years. Moreover, at a relative level, we can speculate regarding the answers to these questions, such as "I was abused as a child," "I was emotionally neglected," "There must be something wrong with the biology or chemistry of my brain," "The socio-economic situation in which I live is oppressive," "I am discriminated against because of my culture" or "My husband/wife/partner is inattentive/crazy/abusive/an alcoholic, etc."

Each of these explanations for why I am suffering in the here-and-now does have at least some validity – but only as correlations, not as causes. When we consider causes, we must move from relative correlations (that is, what has, in some ways, been apparently related to my suffering along the way) to the absolute. And the absolute answer to any "why" question is the same: Because the entire universe has systemically produced these events and conditions – the good and the bad – at the place and time you (and each of us) call "I." What's more, asking why it has done - and is doing – these things can only be answered "Because this is the will of the one Self – also known as the consciousness which is at the very center of all form and within which the universe exists."

So also, discovering possible correlations – often in the past, sometimes in the present – of your suffering, while interesting and even compelling, has no capacity to actually alleviate your suffering. If delving into the question "why?" could lead to the resolution of your suffering, then you probably would not be reading this book.

Instead, therefore, let's look at our suffering – whether it appears that we are the perpetrators of our own misery, the victims of others, or neither, or both – from the biggest picture possible, so to speak. Let's at least consider the possibility that our suffering *needs* to be happening to us – that it indeed has been produced by, or is the manifestation of – the whole of this ecosytemic universe. Let's then be willing to accept our suffering, to work with it rather than trying to get rid of it. Let's, in short, be willing to consider the possibility that our suffering has meaning and that there is an ultimate purpose to it. Additionally, there is no need either for looking to others for salvation or for pointing at others in blame. Let's instead find what grace or gifts there are for us in our suffering.

If we are willing to look for the life lesson we are being presented with in, by and through our suffering, then we are well-positioned to move forward spiritually as expansion in awareness is both the cause and effect of suffering. Moreover, as we actually discover the grace that is at the heart of suffering, suffering begins to recede. Suffering, after all, is not an end in itself and is not gratuitous; when suffering's purpose is realized – and that purpose, again, is greater awareness of who I am – then the need for suffering proportionately declines.

We are thus free to simply, as Eckhart Tolle often puts it, "accept the form this present moment is taking." Put another way, we are free to go with whatever is happening, whether what is happening be emotional, mental, social, vocational, physical and, in many cases, all of these dimensions of our human experience are affected simultaneously. We finally come to the point that, instead of resisting suffering, which, as we have seen, only increases suffering, we allow suffering to simply be, thereby, paradoxically, neutralizing it.

When we non-resistantly come out on the other side of suffering, we realize that our expanded consciousness actually required our ordeals. And that it could have been accomplished no other way.

❖

Chapter 20

The Myth of the One Final Answer

However unconsciously, I was once convinced that, if only I could find the once-and-for-all approach, worldview, attitude, mental gimmick or method, that I would be free and in the clear. But as my desperate attempts to use every spiritual insight I received from within as a "tool" that would work in any and all circumstances inevitably failed, I began to despair that anything, however extraordinary the insight was upon which it was built, could ever provide me direction, save me from anxiety or guide me though ever-changing life situations.

I finally came to the realization that there is truly nothing to hang onto – including any and all spiritual insights – and that there is thus no one final answer which can lift me above the uncertainty and imperfection of daily life and its constant fray. Of equal importance, I came to realize that no one final answer is actually necessary, either.

Yet, is there a spiritual seeker who hasn't, at one time or another, believed in what I call the "Myth of the One Final Answer"? And should we be surprised by this?

We seek, when you really get down to it, depth-level security, and this search is not in itself a problem. But we assume, from the perspective of our delusional human condition, that this security must come in the form of something to which we can cling, such as a teaching, a method, a set of steps or techniques, an attitude or an affirmation. But, once again, the paradoxical truth is that the tighter we hold on the more insecure we become.

As implied above, this is not an indictment against the search for security – only against the methods we use in attempting to create it and the unconscious and delusional assumptions about what real security actually is and upon what it is based.

As Alan Watts states in his book, *The Wisdom of Insecurity*:

To discover the ultimate Reality of life – the Absolute, the Eternal, God – you must cease to try to grasp it in the form of idols. These idols....are our beliefs, our cherished preconceptions of the truth, which block the unreserved opening of mind and heart to reality.[1]

In short, there is no one final answer and never will be. But there doesn't need to be one, either. What a relief it is to be free, from one moment to the next, without pre-set demands as to what this moment must contain or how situations that present themselves in the now moment must evolve or what outcomes must manifest themselves. What serenity to approach each new situation without a fear-based strategy for coping with it. We no longer need guardedness, defensiveness, hyper-vigilance or the rigidity that proceeds from out of heavy pain.

Instead, we come to realize that it is safe to live with spontaneity, abandon, trust and love, allowing the "chips to fall where they may," as the saying goes. The shadow – once so dense, heavy and dark – begins to lift and the light shines from within.

And all without having to find, or produce, the one final answer.

---

[1] Watts, Alan W. (1951). *The Wisdom of Insecurity: A Message for an Age of Anxiety*, p. 26.

✿

Chapter 21

The Dynamics of Faith

What is faith, besides a 5-letter word? To what sort of phenomenon does that word point? Faith, properly and dynamically understood, refers not to intellectual assent to religious tenets or to cognitively-based and language-expressed beliefs, but to an event and an experience.

When experienced authentically, it becomes clear to the human subject that faith, first of all, is a gift. It is not, in other words, an attitude that I have conjured up or created. Faith, moreover, is a "letting go" rather than a clinging onto, the result of a collapse of will-based effort rather than a decision of the will and, in its lack of content, is essentially synonymous with the word "trust."

Faith thus "happens" where it happens, appears without a specific cause and can no more be made to happen in oneself than it can be made to happen in another. Faith comes, therefore, from the "inside-out," from "within," as it were, and represents the arrival of a new structure of being, a new consciousness, a new self.

For genuine faith lifts consciousness, you could say, to a level above and beyond identification with ego or the supposed person, such identification being the centerpiece of conventional consciousness. The coming of faith is, indeed, synonymous with what has been called "self-transcendence" or "trans-egoic" consciousness.

I am, by way of faith, introduced to my true Self, which is

universal, undivided, uninterrupted, boundary-less awareness or consciousness itself. I become acquainted with this presence, which grounds my existence, and realize, moreover, that this presence/consciousness is who I ultimately and truly am. Awareness becomes, in this way, aware of itself and thus fulfills its very purpose in human beings – to come together with, or return to, itself.

Faith is awareness which no longer is compelled to look away from itself – as if there were anything other than itself to which to look ! – for completion, contentment and fulfillment. Faith thus represents an "easing back into" oneself and the "withdrawing of projections," as Jung termed it, that characterizes the liberated state of consciousness – that is, consciousness which is no longer in bondage to the compulsiveness of the human condition. Faith is the omega point, the end of the search, the overcoming of ego and its correlate, the world.

Interestingly – and confounding to some – faith understood in this way is not faith *in* anyone or anything. It is a simple, non egoic relaxation which happens entirely by itself (or "by the grace of God," which means precisely the same thing).

Thus it is that if you believe you don't have faith – or have too little of it – there is no point whatsoever in attempting to directly increase or produce faith. Ironically, such efforts would, in that they represent attempts at changing one's consciousness by and through a decision of the will, constitute a decided *lack* of faith, faith being the radical acceptance of what is happening now, including one's supposed lack of faith.

But faith is not synonymous with passivity. The consciousness rooted in faith is as capable of taking action without hesitation when needed as it is of pulling back and allowing things to be as they are when nothing can or need be done about them. In both cases – action and passivity – consciousness rooted in faith remains uninvested in outcomes and remains non-interfering with what needs to be. And what needs to be is *both* what one does *and* what happens – that is, the voluntary and the involuntary, which are opposite aspects of the universal process (or "Tao").

You are free to notice those moments during which faith is present. But there is no need to cling to those moments. Becoming more aware of them, in effect, more deeply roots consciousness in faith. This is the transformation for which you seek.

❊

Chapter 22

You Don't "Got To." You "Get To"

I don't think I will ever forget a client saying, in a moment of crystal clear insight, "You know what? It seems that I don't 'got to' do anything. Awareness is already here. But I 'get to' consciously choose to experience that awareness anytime, anywhere."

Many years later I still marvel at this simple but profound insight. Inherent in the statement is a clear shift in perspective. My client was no longer viewing reality and himself from the limited standpoint of the body/mind organism and the false identity this position implies. Instead, he'd moved to the absolute perspective of awareness itself, within which the body, the ego which supposedly "inhabits" the body and, indeed, all form exists.[1]

What's more, from that unlimited perspective, there is nothing that stands in the way of direct experience of awareness by awareness. You don't "got to" do anything. Instead, you "get to" move forward in *this* moment – now, without further waiting or preparation – and in perfect freedom.

Conditioned thought patterns. Entanglement with the world and the false consciousness the world implies. These phenomena almost guarantee that I will assume that I "got to" do this, believe that, feel this, and then – maybe – I'll enjoy liberation. Doesn't success in attaining worldly goals require careful planning, preparation, doing this and believing all the right things? How on earth could spiritual liberation be any different? In fact, not needing to do anything to earn or attain spiritual freedom is even a bit insulting. Who has the right to take this issue out of my own hands? To accomplish it as I see fit?

My own hands. As I see fit. Ego demands that enlightenment be its own project. Who else is there, after all, that will take the project on? Whose project is this after all?

In truth, ego fears its demise. If enlightenment is not an ego project and happens "tathata" (Sanskrit for "of itself"), then an entirely new dimension has pushed ego (or the person) to the margins and, as Jung once put it, has "created a new center." What's more, that center, as it is decidedly *not* the egoic "I" or "me," is threatening almost beyond words. It might even mean the elimination of me as I have known myself.

Again the questions might arise: "Who or what am I anyway? Am I this new dimension over which I seem to have no actual control and which has come without conscious invitation into consciousness? Or am I still Karl, the guy I've always assumed I am?"

No, much better to continue in old consciousness and to "push away" this new dimension. To deny it. To continue insisting that I must "work on myself" or my defects, prepare, do this, believe that, pray for help. Remain in control, in other words.

Eventually, when the bottom is finally hit, one comes to realize how illusory this control always was. Then might even come panic. "Is it too late to make friends with this new center before it kills me altogether? Can I yet be saved? Can I still find refuge and be set free? Might I end up going insane or committing suicide first?"

But it's okay. The whole struggle and drama has been the play of God. All is indeed well. You're alright. Despite the fear, you haven't become dysfunctional. It's just that you, consciously as the Self now, will be playing the former role in the universal drama *knowing* that it is just a temporary role.

I am – and always have been – that new dimension that seemed so frightening, but which now has come to know itself by and through this particular body/mind. I don't "got to" anymore. I "get to." I get to move on knowing my true identity.

Could anything be more extraordinary than this?

---

[1] This writer takes the position, of course, that ego, as such, is an illusion (entirely non-existent, in other words). The body/mind certainly exists, though, as an expression of the Self, it lacks reality in and of itself. Yet, both ego and body/mind are forms (though of differing types), in that even an illusion, as it appears to exist, is perceived by consciousness.

✿

Chapter 23

What are You Waiting For?

Spiritual seekers, by virtue of being, or defining themselves as, spiritual seekers, are seeking something. But what? Peace? Serenity? Life purpose or meaning? And, of course, you believe that you currently possess or experience none, or precious little, of these things.

Growing awareness eventually reveals to us that, though perhaps we no longer crave more money, a bigger house or car, a better partner, worldly recognition, more drugs or alcohol and the like, we still suffer from a nagging anxiety that we need more in the way of spirituality or the gifts we assume will come to us by way of spirituality. We have, in short, become spiritual addicts and are convinced we need more.

But, you protest, "What is spiritual growth if it's not a growth in the amount, or level, of spirituality you 'have' or experience?" "I need," you may continue, "more happiness, awakening, enlightenment, surrender, realization, liberation. I obviously don't have enough. I haven't arrived yet."

We may – and I recall this poignantly in my own life – eventually even eschew searching for these goodies, having perhaps come to believe that, since I cannot obtain or achieve them, I must instead wait patiently for them to arrive on their own.

I recall interpreting this latter shift in approach as representing a great breakthrough, and, in a relative sense, it was. It is indeed critically important that we come to accept our (or ego's) incapacity and inability to lay hold of that for which we have been longing. That the active, even compulsive, striving and trying eventually exhausts itself is undeniably a good thing.

But the outcome I was no longer actively pursuing had simply become the result for which I was now waiting. And, as we have seen, *both* active attempts at achieving *and* passive waiting are invested in the future and so pulled me away from consciousness of the now. "What I can't get actively," reasons ego, "I'll get passively." As noted earlier, activity and passivity are thus two sides of the same coin.

But what if I don't need the coin? What if I come to realize that both active attempts at achieving deeper spirituality and passive waiting for deeper spirituality to arrive – in that both strategies clearly imply that I do not believe that I currently possess deep enough spirituality – are unnecessary as I *already have* deep spirituality by virtue of my birthright as a human (or, you could say, by virtue of my already being the Self in disguise)? What if the now so opens up to me that I finally come to consciously realize that there is nothing other than now and that I am thus free to go deeply into it? What if I thus come to realize that what might be called the "horizontal" dimension of looking forward to a future when I'll be at peace can be replaced by a "vertical" dimension in which I am free to go deeply into the present moment?

My experience has made it abundantly clear to me that the answer to these questions is simple: I realize that I need neither to strive nor to wait. I have all the spirituality I will ever need right here, right now as the now is limitless. In fact, I never will have "more" spirituality than I have right now. I am right now as free from the compulsion to have more spirituality as I am free from the compulsion to acquire more material wealth or the compulsion to drink, drug, act out sexually, overwork, gamble, overeat or whatever ways the human condition might have manifested itself in me. I don't, in short, need to be addicted to anything, including spirituality.

Here, then, is another extraordinary paradox: Awakening is the realization that no awakening is necessary. Surrender is the realization that no surrender is necessary. Liberation is the realization that no liberation is necessary. All of these are *already present* and always have been. "...there is no realization" writes John Wheeler. "Nothing new is brought in. The key is not some new attainment, but simply clarifying what our real nature is."[1]

For what event are you waiting? What do you expect to find or attain? You could search or wait your entire life and that imagined event that you believe to be in the future will never arrive and will never occur. Your clinging to desired outcomes will never result in your freedom.

Fortunately you don't need what you already have. Simply notice the abundance that is here and now. Feel it. Observe it. Witness it. Be aware of it. Fact is, you *are* it.

And that is all one needs to know.

---

[1] Wheeler, John (2007). *You Were Never Born*, p. 116.

❈

Chapter 24

The New Self

Normal (meaning "the norm," or the usual and typical) human consciousness, as we have discussed, is characterized by a deeply conditioned and unquestioned assumption that I am a "person" or a "self" with a name and a history that "inhabits" a human body. The pronoun "I," along with my name, is believed to thus refer to this supposed entity, which often feels centered more or less in the head. I assume this supposed entity, often called the soul, to be who I am, my essential identity.

In some humans – including probably the present reader of this text – this deeply conditioned assumption regarding essential identity is being shaken by the spontaneous awakening of that aspect of overall consciousness which generally remains out of conscious awareness.

The sudden realization at the conscious level that there is "something happening," that there is a "rising up" from within, so to speak, of "I know not what," tends to throw one's sense of identity into crisis. Who or what is this "other" that seems to be "coming up" apparently from the depths?

As a counselor, I know that the first experience of awakening varies considerably and can be quite highly disconcerting. Some people are seized by perplexity. Others – such as myself at one time – are thrown into panic. Still others, willing to let go, feel a coming of peace they'd never before experienced.

Whatever the cognitive/emotional response, the awakening of the spiritual dimension, initiated by that dimension itself, represents the beginning of a process that Carl Jung, as noted earlier, referred to as the creation of a "new center" of consciousness. Ego, which is another name for the conventional sense of the fictional, personal self, is pushed off center as a new sense of identity gradually (in most cases) takes its place.

Once established, the new center, or Self, expands while ego, now unwillingly de-centered, continues to gradually weaken. In my own – and, I think, in most peoples' – experience, this expansion of the new center and the corresponding decline of ego happens processively, though not continuously at the same rate. Leaps forward happen followed by long periods of consolidation and integration. But again, once spiritual awakening begins, it does not stop no matter how long the body/mind lives.

As always, I am free to watch and enjoy the expansion of the light of spiritual awareness, the new center or Self within, all the while knowing that it is happening by itself (or "by the grace of God," which, as mentioned earlier, means the same thing).

And what will we see when we watch? Here it is instructive to consider the words of St. Paul in his New Testament letter to the Galatians (5:22-23). What he calls the "fruit of the spirit" includes love, joy, peace, patience, kindness, goodness, faithfulness, gentleness and self-control. Evelyn Underhill, the great British writer on mysticism, called the fruits of the spirit:

> ...*those dispositions, those ways of thinking, speaking and acting which are brought forth in us, gradually but inevitably, by the pressure of divine love in our souls. They all spring from that one root.*[1]

A new center. The new creature in Christ. The new Self. These are very different words and metaphors, proceeding from out of differing conceptual schemas, but which point to the same phenomenon. That phenomenon is happening in and by you who read these pages.

---

[1] Underhill, Evelyn (1942). *Fruits of the Spirit – Light of Christ – Abba,* p. 6.

❁

Chapter 25

"Make Yourselves Very Small"

When Angela of Foligno, one of the most profound of the medieval mystics and author of "Visions of the Being of God," was on her deathbed, those gathered round her asked for a last teaching from her. She stated simply, "Make yourselves small. Make yourselves very small." [1]

This theme of making ego – or allowing ego to become – small is a central theme in esoteric traditions from many cultures and religions all round the world. Here we further develop that theme by considering the relationship between "ego" (or, again, the conventional, deeply conditioned and unconscious assumption regarding who I am) and "God," or, to use non-religious terms which have appeared in this text and which refer to the same dimension of reality, the formless, consciousness or awareness.

Or is it even a relationship, as western religion usually has assumed, between a person, Karl, for example, and a supreme being? Maybe you are more inclined toward the eastern (or "quantum," or non-dual) perspective and so prefer to view your own identity and formlessness as being ultimately identical. "Atman is Brahman," as the Hindus have, for many millennia, claimed. This is the central theme, of course, of the present book.

Whatever one's ontology – advaita (non-dual) or dualistic – I think we can all agree that spiritual people through the ages have emphasized that it is "something other" than who they had typically thought themselves to be that is the source of depth-level connection, liberation and creative work in the world.

Now one may conceive of this "other" in western terms, as many have done and still do, and claim that it is God and not I, who saves, redeems and restores. One may, instead, insist that this "other" only *seems* to be other and that it – the formless, Brahman, God or whatever you wish to call this dimension – is really your own deepest, most authentic Self, or Atman.

Either way, this "getting ego out of God's way," or a neutralizing or an eliminating of the person so that, in becoming transparent to the ground of being, the ground is able to shine through, is at the heart of spiritual teaching from all ages and cultures.

But a question usually arises at this point which goes something like this: "These descriptions – east and west – are all very good as far as they go. But how do I get ego, or myself, out of the way?" We thus return to the question of agency, which, in its dogged persistence in most of us, is worth further consideration here.

Moreover, the question re-focuses us away from description and once again on the prescriptive. And, in my view, however inevitable it is that we confront this issue, we may as well accept that the question is fraught, as we have seen, with potential problems, generally created by the mind.

First, the question quite obviously proceeds from out of the assumption that "I" refers to an individual person, an assumption which has been called "egoic consciousness."

Now, for a moment, assuming that ego, or "I, Karl," for example, actually does exist as a separate will, how do I get myself out of the way? How, as the Zen master asked, "does ego eliminate ego"? It is clear that any and all attempts which I might make to get myself out of the way actually only puts me in the way all the more. Even more attention is focused, in other words, on what is perceived as being in the way and this inevitably is a distraction from the consciousness (or God) which we would have shine forth without the obstruction of ego. Moreover, this phenomenon becomes, as we have seen, self-perpetuating in that the more I, as the person, try to eliminate the obstruction of the person – which thus only increases personal identity, or ego – the more I must apply effort to rid myself of the person! All the while, of course, I do not realize that what I am attempting to get rid of is a mind-made assumption which, though it may in some illusory sense "exist," has no actual reality.

Obviously we are off on the wrong track here. But being off on the wrong track is a given when one's basic assumptions as to who one is are faulty.

Most often the futility of getting rid of ego must run its course and bring the seeker to a crisis of some sort before this is seen. And yet, as William Blake assures us "The fool who persists in his folly will become wise." Simply see for yourself, in other words, where your effort to eliminate ego leads you. Eventually it will lead to despair of your ever breaking free of ego, which means perpetually standing in your own way.

Are you tired of this yet? If you truly are, then you will come to realize that the whole strategic affair has been completely unnecessary.[2]

For it turns out that there is no need whatsoever to "get myself out of the way" as even the feeling, impression, perception or sensation of a separate "I" are *themselves* forms which exist – however temporarily – within the seamless and boundaryless whole that is awareness.

Thus it is that awareness *must* be who you are. After all, awareness is the one phenomenon which cannot be reduced down to a more fundamental reality. I, Karl, when examined, simply becomes a temporary ripple in the larger stream of consciousness. But to what can you reduce consciousness itself down? Fact is, consciousness is actually irreducible. Indeed, you need consciousness even to attempt a reduction of consciousness! Reduction simply can't be done to consciousness itself. Consciousness is simply what is – eternally and necessarily.

In short, you *are* that irreducible dimension we call "consciousness." How could you be anything else when anything else – all form, in other words, including the human body/mind – turns out, in the end, to be completely lacking in subjective consciousness?

Again, the truth of the simple statement of ultimate realization – "Tat tvam asi," "You are that" – rings clearly. You are consciousness. The true, ultimate and absolute you is eternal, formless and spaceless. Thus it is that, as has been stated several times in this text, you are *both* the "space" within which all forms exist *and* the consciousness which is at the heart, or which grounds, all form. You are the watcher, in other words, *and* the essence of all that is being watched.

There is, to summarize, only you. There is no other.

[1] Underhill, Evelyn (1942). *Fruits of the Spirit – Light of Christ – Abba*, p. 36.

[2] And yet, at the same time entirely necessary in another sense, as everything that happens is, in this other sense, necessary, having its source in the will of the One, or the whole of this ecosytemic universe.

❋

Chapter 26

Don't Look, Don't Grasp

How vividly I recall, at age 21, the initial arrival of depth-level joy. The serenity was deep, rich and nothing like anything I'd ever experienced. Yet, how quickly the experience faded away after other people, circumstances and worldly concerns came, once again, to take priority over it.

I spent the next several years trying to get that experience back. And if there is one thing I learned from that subsequent search it is that there is no point in trying to get the "cloud 9" experience back. If it's gone, then it's gone. You may as well accept it.

But that last line, especially the key word "accept," is a clue that, along with the "bad news" that the peace which had come and which had all too quickly gone away cannot be recovered, there is good news. The good news is that I don't actually *need* to recover that peace as acceptance that the peace is gone *is* that same peace. A simple truth, yes. But it took me years to learn it.

Indeed, if I were now to offer assistance on this issue of "re-gaining" a sense of serenity that has apparently "gone away," I would suggest that there is no need to re-gain it. In fact, to even try re-gaining it causes that very peace to remain out of reach. As Shankara stated, "Fire can burn everything except itself." Attempting to grab hold of security is like trying to make fire burn itself.

Why is this? As stated elsewhere in this text, it is impossible to see the seer, and the seer – the one attempting to see or the very phenomenon of seeing – implies that what you are trying to get is what is doing the trying. One may as well give that strategy up as an utter futility. Nathan Gill writes:

> *What has been sought all along is found to be none other than this which is the seeking. The ultimate goal or prize turns out to be what already is. There is nothing and no one to find. There is awareness with no one being aware....There is nothing and no one...You are, and always have been, completely awake, aware and present, but merely mesmerized by your own cosmic play.*[1]

As was suggested earlier in this text, doesn't this strike you as actually being good news? If grasping after, or looking for, the "ultimate prize" is futile because what you are looking for is that which is doing the looking, then I don't need to do it! What a relief to have this burden lifted from me. I'm finally free from having to compulsively attempt the impossible.

Turns out that what we've always wanted has been right there all along. Right under our noses. In fact, it can't NOT be there. *What it is I've been looking for is, in fact, who I deeply am.* Knowledge of this truth sets me free as nothing else could.

---

[1] Gill, Nathan (2004). *Already Awake: Dialogues with Nathan Gill*, p. 26.

✿

Chapter 27

Enlightenment is the Realization that No Enlightenment is Needed

The title of this chapter first appeared in the body of chapter 23 and is being cited here so as to provide further consideration of this important truth.

To most of us spiritual seekers, the word "enlightenment" possesses a highly compelling allure. We might imagine ourselves as "someday" being enlightened and assume that we then would no longer experience our current, possibly high, levels of emotional distress. We would be at peace, enjoying unending bliss and serenity.

We want this. And we are willing to do almost anything to attain it. This is all quite understandable.

We also imagine that becoming enlightened will finally prove to us and to others our obvious superiority over other people, whom we have, often enough, regarded as fools. These unconscious, superficial and immature child-adults, who, in their self-indulgence, have always taken the easy way and have been, moreover, rewarded by a jaded and spiritually dead world for so doing. Yes, they all, at last, will be forced to acknowledge their dullness, lack of integrity and frivolity compared to us, the enlightened ones.

Ah, enlightenment. What a way to get "one up" on others and the world and to exercise the power for which many of us have secretly longed.

Now there's nothing "wrong" with these desires, attitudes or cravings. They have long, I am convinced, constituted significant aspects of the "shadow side" of spiritual people. They thus indicate and expose an unconsciousness in us that many of us, this writer included, have been all too unwilling to have brought into the light of conscious awareness.

"You mean I can't even harbor feelings of rage, resentment and injustice against the great masses of people whose very existence seems to mock and marginalize my high-minded and earnest search for truth? Don't they know how much I could help them? Yet, they ignore me. And now I'm being told that I – *I*, the genuine, the pure, a rare exemplar of serious values in this dark and benighted world – am suffering from unconsciousness?!"

It's all just too much.

I recall simply refusing to accept what amounted to a suggestion that my "humility" was largely false. "Damn it, I *am* enlightened – or at least well on my way there – and no further dispelling of the shadow is necessary in me! In others, yes. In spades, in fact. But not in me."

Oh, the pain that was driving this. Age old pain. Pain originating in my childhood, when I had begun to feel so misunderstood – and, of course, so alienated as a result. Around this pain had been constructed defenses that hid ego's alliance with the shadow. What's more, behind those defenses no light of awareness was permitted. Assumptions about my own identity that lay behind those walls went unquestioned, unexamined and had become deeply conditioned. Spirituality was thus made to conform to the old self's structure of existence. At least at first.

Thus it was that, to some extent, my early and deep interest in spirituality itself had been drawn into the service of the shadow in me. Spirituality had been co-opted as further justification for my deep resentfulness at a world which seemed to daily rebuke me and all that I believed I was and in which I had become personally invested.

I, the righteous, self-denying one, could thus bitterly, perhaps even heroically, stand against the world with an inner sneer that was covered over by a "Mr. Nice Guy" persona.

Again, the deep pain at the center of those urgent self-defensive and unconscious strategies today seems extraordinary to me. Moreover, the delusional thinking, rooted in deep unconsciousness, poisoned even the nascent spiritual inclination rising up within me.

Fortunately, though, the light of consciousness, as we know, continues to brighten and expand, eventually illuminating hidden and dark corners of consciousness.

What's more, among the secrets we are eventually "let in on" is that the crafty ways which ego, in alliance with the shadow, has framed spirituality and the Self-realization process is highly distorting. We come to see that true enlightenment, far from being an ego-aggrandizing and self-protective strategy, is actually a *freedom from* all the "works and ways" of ego and the shadow.

In fact, true enlightenment is the realization, when the blinders are taken from our inner eyes, that no enlightenment is actually necessary. No "special experience" – moksha, nirvana, liberation – need be striven for or made into an ultimate goal. No awakening, transformation or shift in consciousness, as we have imagined them, need happen. Quoting, again, Nathan Gill:

> *You are Consciousness, oneness, all that is, the source*
> *and appearance of all....nothing needs to change for this*
> *to be so. No awakening or enlightenment is needed...*[1]

Or, to say the exact same thing, the realization that no transformation, enlightenment, shift or awakening need happen *is*, in
fact, the transformation, enlightenment, shift and awakening that
we have so ardently been seeking. Ego has, in this manner, been
de-commissioned and has no role whatsoever.

Ego, of course, will protest. "But how do I make what is happening at that deepest level of me conscious?" it asks. "How do I
become aware of it?" Ego continues to thus insist that it be in charge
of the project. Indeed, as we have seen, ego cannot be eliminated
by trying to eliminate it. "How can washing your hands in muddy
water make clean your muddy hands?" as the Zen master asked.
We have arrived, therefore, at a level of non-duality and paradox
which ego cannot contain, understand or control.

The answer, then, to the above question regarding bringing
awareness to the deepest level of myself must be: You need not
bring what is happening at that level of yourself to awareness. It
can't be done at any rate because any attempt to become aware of
transformed consciousness would be fundamentally and necessarily egoic. And ego, it turns out, only seeks to block realization.

At the same time, we, at this point, are free to approach the
issue from an entirely new angle. Instead of viewing the prospect
of directly experiencing new consciousness as implying something
which I "must do," I, in perfect liberty, and if I am ready for such
profound simplicity, may notice, be aware of and observe new
consciousness. What I, of course, will eventually realize is that
new consciousness is observing itself.

Witness and what is witnessed are, as we have seen, the same. I have "come together with myself," as it were. The inner divide has been overcome. The primal conflict between I and myself is brought to an end. That between conscious and unconscious is over. That between myself and other is transcended. I know who I am.

Yet, expect what remains of egoic energy to attempt "butting itself in" at this point and saying something such as "Yes, but I still don't feel/experience/ know/realize this."

One's response to ego's continual struggle for centrality can take the form of non-reactivity, or "no response," as it becomes ever more clear that ego's protests are based in the illusion – an illusion which one has begun seeing through – that one lacks what one desires so intensely. No lack actually exists. Thus it is that, while one cannot directly stop ego's claims and complaints, one need no longer be deceived by them. One is free to continue simply watching and witnessing. Even when distraction away from awareness happens, no effort need be undertaken to correct this as one remains the witness even when distracted. The re-awakening from distraction, which happens by itself, is, again, sufficient. One's consciousness becomes, therefore, ever simpler and free of conflict and anxiety.

Can life in this world be any more fulfilling than this?

---

[1] Gill, Nathan (2004). *Already Awake: Dialogues with Nathan Gill*, p. 18).

✿

Chapter 28

"I am the Light of the World"

In the 8th chapter of the Gospel of St. John, Jesus says "I am the light of the world." The institutional church has, as we know, interpreted the pronoun "I" in this statement as referring to the man, Jesus of Nazareth, called the Christ. In fact, if there is one thing upon which all the many and various otherwise competing denominations of the Christian religion can and do agree it is that Jesus was a unique God-man, different in kind from every other person who has ever, or ever will, live.

But realizing one's true identity as the Self enables one to perceive many issues and phenomena from an entirely new perspective, probably most particularly the truth as to what or to whom the pronoun "I" ultimately refers.

"I," undoubtedly one of the most frequently used words in the English language, typically is assumed, as has been discussed, to refer to the separate body/mind which I supposedly am. Thus it is that egoic consciousness lies at the very root of language and language, in turn, reinforces the deep, conditioned, unexamined and unconscious assumption that I am a separate person with a separate will that "inhabits," as it were, a human body.

Language itself, then, constitutes a veil which hides from us our true identity. Yet, once this veil is lifted, we become privy to the previously hidden nature of reality, including who we really are.

Jesus (whether he literally existed as a historical figure, as most assume, or whether he is largely or entirely mythological, as some have suggested[1]) can be viewed as a human by and through whom the Self came to fully realize itself as the universal one Self to which the pronoun "I" ultimately refers. From this perspective, Jesus is not unique in kind but in degree.

But if this happened in Jesus – or if the phenomenon is symbolized mythologically by ancient biblical stories which feature this character – then presumably Self-realization has happened, and continues to happen, by and through other humans, as well.

Could you, the reader, say "I am the light of the world" and mean it sincerely, as Jesus did? Could the writer, Karl Galten, make this same claim?

The fact is that, since the unbroken, boundaryless and timeless consciousness referred to metaphorically as "the light," is, as we have shown, the irreducible element in all experience (to even so much as deny the truth of this statement requires consciousness), then each of us, to emphasize again this point, simply *must* be, at our deepest levels, this consciousness. When realization of this truth occurs, then the statement "I am the light of the world" is plainly evident.

There is but one Self and thus but one I. I am the light of the world. And so are you.

---

[1] See, for examples, the work of Timothy Freke and Peter Gandy, Albert Schweitzer, Gerald Massey, Thomas Harpur and Alvin Boyd Kuhn.

✿

Chapter 29

Reaction is Bondage

Driving home on the freeway can be a harrowing experience in large American cities. It's not unusual for drivers to follow the vehicle just ahead too closely at high speeds or to carelessly and impatiently "cut off," as they change lanes, other drivers. What's more, reactions to these dangerous incidents is often anger, and, at times, even rage.

On my routine drive home one night not long ago a speeding driver roared past me, then swerved quickly into my lane, resulting in my needing to brake suddenly so as to avoid a collision. Rage appeared in consciousness.

Instantly the teaching came through directly from within: To react is to lose freedom and to be distracted from the peace of consciousness.

Indeed, "non-reactivity" – a word which points to the same experience as do the words "detachment," "acceptance of the present moment" and "allowing" – is a central theme in much spiritual teaching. Essentially, non-reactivity is the capacity to remain "disentangled," one might say, in what happens, either within oneself or without. It is based on a firm conviction that no such entanglement is necessary and can in no way rectify or resolve any situation or set of circumstances in which one may find oneself. "Let whatever happens happen" and "Whatever you're doing, do it fully, and let the chips fall where they may" might represent brief summaries of non-reactive, detached living. The ancient Chinese Taoist teacher, Chuang-Tzu, put it this way: "The perfect man employs his mind as a mirror. It grasps nothing. It refuses nothing. It receives, but does not keep."

Protests arise, though, in many, if not most, of us against the idea of non-reactivity.

As noted earlier, a common protest that I, in my counseling practice, hear quite frequently is that non-reactivity sounds or feels synonymous with passivity. And passivity, perhaps especially among those of us in whom ego has been very strong, is strictly taboo. "You mean we should never try changing anything? That we should allow ourselves to be victimized? Or settle for marginal outcomes?"

These objections, as always, are understandable. But they are also based upon a misunderstanding of true non-reactivity.

Passivity, as we have seen, is a type of strategy. Its opposite, of course, is activity, which is another type of strategy. Both passivity and activity are designed to reach particular outcomes and are thus highly invested in future. In fact, also as has been discussed earlier, it is not unusual among spiritual seekers, when told that active pursuing of enlightenment cannot ever issue in actual enlightenment, for active pursuing then to become its opposite – passivity.

But passivity becomes only an alternative way by which ego remains in control. "What I can't get actively, I will get passively." We are thus, because of this future emphasis and attachment to an imagined outcome – enlightenment – just as far from enlightenment as when we were actively pursuing it. Enlightenment, after all, is now, not in the future.

But detachment, acceptance of the present moment or, if you prefer, non-reactivity, involves an over-emphasis on neither activity nor passivity and is free from the future emphasis of both. Detachment is based on a conscious "going with" the form the now is currently taking and thus is not a means to arrive at an imagined better end or future. Detachment is oriented vertically downward and within, to use a spacial metaphor, toward a deeper awareness of, and conscious connection to, now.

Detachment, also, therefore, includes freedom to be active when a particular situation calls for action to be taken toward the resolution of the many practical issues which constantly arise in the now. I take action, for example, when I apply for entrance into a university, greet a new client, drive to work, hug my daughter, apply for a job, cut the grass or advocate in some way or another for myself or others. Expressing my thoughts or emotions are also actions I may take. At the same time, I am free to do nothing if a situation cannot be changed, if I need to rest or to disengage from relationships or other social role functions in which I might have become, in unconsciousness, entangled. Our little rule might be: "If you don't know what to do, it's best not to do anything, at least until it becomes clear what to do."

Detachment, or non-reactivity, thus includes both action and inaction and essentially involves freedom from the compulsion to cling to either pole.

Detachment is thus synonymous with freedom. It is remaining conscious of one's distinction, as the witness, from the world of form of all types, both "inner" and "outer." It is a self-containment that is of the essence of peace and it maintains what Eckhart Tolle calls the "space" between the witness, on the one hand, and what is witnessed, on the other. "Only the thoroughly detached soul is free," as "The Mirror of Simple Souls" puts it.

Along these same lines, Carl Jung described what he termed the "process of individuation" as, among other things, involving the "withdrawal of projections," as was discussed earlier. This latter phrase, in turn, implies detachment and becoming "conscious of consciousness," as I have called it elsewhere in this text, and which is a correlate of detachment.

Moreover, one seems eventually to question whether distraction from consciousness is actually necessary. Is it necessary to become enthralled with form? To get lost in thinking? To focus on either the past or future? To react?

For instance, through obsessive thinking, am I increasing the likelihood of good things happening and bad things not happening? Is thinking continuously not itself a distraction from consciousness? And, if it is, of what benefit is it? As Jesus says in the New Testament book of St. Matthew (6:27): "... which of you by being anxious can add one cubit to his span of life?"

This is not to say that distraction by thought ceases altogether in most of us. I, for one, can attest to still becoming distracted, at times, by this care or that, this concern or that, this fear/regret/desire or that. But – and here's what has changed – I have begun questioning whether distraction is actually necessary. The answer: No, it is not. Thus it is that distraction is no longer being "driven," as it had been, by an unconscious sense of necessity and is thus gradually "slowing down" through not being constantly reinforced.

Though distraction still happens, in other words, I have come to realize that it serves no necessary purpose. This realization has removed from the distraction the sense of urgency that had for years driven and fueled obsessive/compulsive patterns of thought and action. The disappearance of this continuous fueling, in other words, has led to a reduction in the frequency, intensity and duration of distraction. I expect this process to continue.

Awareness, once planted and however gradually, replaces thinking. No matter how important mind and thinking may remain in the realm of practical affairs and problem solving, it is safe to stop using it for purposes it can never fulfill. It is safe to withdraw from thinking and to instead be open to what's happening in the now, both "within" and in the social and natural environment "around" me. The human mind, mediated by logic and rationality and often driven by fear, is transcended and, in its place comes spirit, mediated by intuition.

The nature of this new consciousness, moreover, is non-reactive, allowing and open – while remaining capable, yes, of both action and thought when needed. Interestingly, thought, when not dominant, actually seems to function at a significantly higher level than when hindered by the interfering and intrusive ego, which is inevitably created when one's identity is entangled in thought. Similarly, one's social role functioning, in general, actually improves when one is free from the heaviness of ego, that "me" which I had always thought was so central to effective living.

To summarize then: Non-reactivity is egolessness and, therefore, freedom. Detachment is rooted in the capacity to consciously be the witness to all phenomena and taken in by none. It is living in, as the scripture says, "righteousness, peace and joy" (Romans 14:17).

Let us end this chapter with a brief quote from a Buddhist poem: "While living in this world, be a dead person, thoroughly dead. Then whatever you do will be right."

❀

Chapter 30

The Truth Cannot be Captured

Oh, how many years did I attempt to "grab hold of" the formula that would wrap truth up in a package of words? The main goal, of course, was the experience of connection, of feeling one with the ground of being, the "shadow side" of which was feeling "one up," if you will, on life and other people. Invulnerable to pain. Untouchable by anyone bent on hurting me. Above it all.

Yet, despite my shadowy, unconscious and perhaps somewhat cynical motives, truth was, in fact, shown to me nonetheless. But not in or by words, concepts or abstractions of any type. Truth sneaked in, as it were, underneath controlling, hyper-vigilant, obsessive ego consciousness and found *me*; I, conventionally and egoically defined, did not find *it*.

But this, naturally, was not enough for me; as usual, I needed more. What followed, therefore, was the inevitable attempt to describe, grasp, capture and "bottle" the gift of grace I had experienced so suddenly as if ego could thereby use it to reproduce the experience at will.

But similar to Mr. Ed, the talking horse in the iconic 1960's situation comedy of the same name, who refused to speak to anyone except his human, Wilbur Post, the deep Self, from which everything, including subtle spiritual teaching and revelations originate, continued to insist that spiritual experience be on *its* terms, not ego's. Indeed, whenever ego attempted clinging to a sublime experience or truth revealed, put it into words, systematize it, make it into a prescription, capture and use it, it seemed to vanish. Like Mr. Ed, the deep Self would not be exploited; but it did seem interested in revealing itself, in seeking connection with layers of itself "closer to the surface," you could say. I, as I knew myself, was apparently its conduit, the means by which it was seeking to express its infinity by and through the finite. I soon realized that the sooner I gave up the attempt to capture it and allow myself to be appropriated in this way, the better. We often use the phrase "the process of realization" to describe this gradual transformation of consciousness, as it initiates and sustains a shift in one's identity from ego to Self. The word "surrender," as it applies to the collapse of egoic efforts, also is commonly applied.

Today, analogous to Wilbur Post, who eventually gave up trying to persuade Mr. Ed to talk with anyone but himself and only then came to cherish his relationship with Ed, I, too, came eventually to "get the picture." I came finally to realize: I may as well give up any and all attempts at capturing spiritual experience for use at a later time or to somehow make it into a prescriptive method. These attempts had only resulted in the insight or experience disappearing. And, if it had then disappeared, was the teaching ever really fully integrated into consciousness or into what we call the personality? Probably not.

Thus it is, as is true most often in matters spiritual, a "getting out of the way," as we have called it, a fading away of the illusion of the separate self that would "appropriate" truths revealed to it, must occur. I come to realize, in other words, that I, at my deepest level, *am,* in fact, the teacher, providing insight to a previously alienated aspect of myself that had mis-identified itself as a "person" named Karl. Teacher and taught are one.

Is there, then, any actual need for me to remember, recount or apply anything? In the now (and where else is it possible to be?) I am complete and whole. Such is the perfection – and perfect adequacy – of now. I am that.

❖

Chapter 31

All "Problems" Originate in Ego

I recall with sharp poignancy the bitter resentment I carried with me as I left my childhood years and made my way, hesitantly, into that wider world of challenge with which we must cope in adolescence.

Other people – particularly my peers – didn't appreciate me as I believed they should. They all seemed so caught up in their own aims – and most often those aims seemed to diverge very significantly from my own. This, in my mind, amounted to an indictment of me and my priorities. Thus was my fear and rage driven and constantly fed.

But, I realize now, that, as usual, I had "put the cart before the horse." It wasn't "they" who were causing my suffering. I, in my mis-identification of myself as a separate, very needy and grossly victimized person, was causing my own suffering, which I then interpreted as originating from the inappropriate behavior of others (Jung called this phenomenon "projection") – "inappropriate" in that, most often, it was in no way directed toward building up, praising and reinforcing my grandiose and insatiable thirst for indulgence.

This cycle is vicious and pernicious. Self-alienation, or the apparent (but unreal, however convincing) division which seems to exist as a central feature of the human condition and which remains outside the realm of conscious awareness, drives the Self on a search for connection with itself which simply cannot be accomplished given the terms upon which the search is based. Moreover, some of us suffer from the human condition more acutely and more extremely than do others.

Here, then, at the point of what is often termed psychopathology and delusional thinking, is opportunity – the Self's opportunity for Self-realization. It is at this point, after all, that patterns of thought, behavior and emotion, because they have gone so far in one direction, can shift and appear, sometimes suddenly, at the opposite end of the pole.

Jung called this phenomenon "enantiodromia," a strange word by which he referred to a dramatic change in the direction of the Self based on its having gone to an extreme in a particular and opposite direction. Mystics have often termed this same event "conversion." A synonymous word much employed in the present work, of course, is "awakening." The Twelve Step movement calls this 180 degree turnabout the "admission of powerlessness," which is forced upon the addict by his having "hit bottom." William Blake's poetic line quoted earlier ,"A fool who persists in his folly will become wise," also captures the essence of this "about face," which marks the onset of what is most often a long and gradual process of personality change, the prerequisite of which is complete egoic failure.

Similarly, in the 12th chapter of St. Paul's second letter to the Corinthians, verse 9, the 1st century mystic writes of divine power being "made perfect in weakness." Jesus refers to this same phenomenon in the 8th chapter of the gospel of St. Luke, verse 47, in which he forgives the sins of a prostitute, and takes the opportunity to point out that those who are forgiven much, love much, "but he who is forgiven little, loves little."

Thus it is that many of us who have been given the gift of depth-level faith and a direct experience of God, and have even come eventually to realize that the words "I" and "God" ultimately point to the same phenomenon, had spent many years searching for healing of the deep divisions within us through this relationship or that, in this philosophy or that, in this activity or that only to become more and more disillusioned as our pain grew with each new disappointment. Moreover, we had, on account of our profound experience of Self-alienation, been vulnerable to the shadow's lies. And it didn't really matter whether it was "our own" shadow or that of "others" – the shadow being ultimately as indivisible as are self and other – that undermined us. We were being consumed "from within" and "from without."

Such is the nature of consciousness that, if it seeks to go "outside itself" for relief from the pain of disconnection from itself, then this very seeking results only in more pain, a downward, self-perpetuating cycle that leads eventually to despair.

How ironic, then, that we who, in our lack of psychological boundaries, had become so hopelessly and unconsciously entangled with others, also become the most lonely and isolated of people. I refer, of course, to what, in modern Twelve Step parlance, is known as "codependence," a much less definable, vague and subtle addiction than most others.

Codependence, or addiction to other people. How "under the radar" this phenomenon tends to be. And how spiritually deadening. At the same time, codependence is itself *indicative* of spiritual deadness, revealing, once again, the vicious cycle of all addiction: Codependence is *both* cause *and* effect of an underlying spiritual condition characterized by the Self's urgent search for itself. Many of us, in fact, have come to see codependence as our primal addiction, preceding any and all addictions which might have come later. In all probability, it is the last of our addictions from which we are liberated.

Freedom from the "bondage of self," an often-quoted phrase in the Step Three prayer from the book, *Alcoholics Anonymous*,[1] implies, among other things, freedom from the bondage of those problematic other people, who've never had the courtesy to determine what it is we want and then to go about fulfilling those wants. Turns out the "bondage of self" is but one side of the coin; bondage to others goes right along with it on the other side.

Oh, the joy of walking through this world not needing to keep one's awareness and attention always on others, as if other apparent "persons" have any more ultimate reality than all the fears, dependencies and projections that had us simmering in rage and resentment all those many years. Instead, we are free to affirm that pure awareness is prior to what appears in it and that I am that pure awareness. This knowledge is entrance into the kingdom of heaven.

---

[1] *Alcoholics Anonymous* (2001). Alcoholics Anonymous World Services, p. 63.

❄

Chapter 32

Are there Stages of Awakening?

Most spiritual seekers and teachers refer to the *process* of spiritual growth or awakening, a concept which brings to mind the possibility of identifying stages or phases of awakening. In fact, and especially in the west since the Middle Ages (if not dating back to the ancient world and the neo-Platonists, such as Plotinus), many notable teachers have offered a kind of "descriptive map" of the process of Self-realization, union with God, deification and the many other language-based pointers to the experience of transformation. St. Teresa's "Seven Degrees of Contemplation" is an example of an attempt to describe the process with the aid of stages or phases.

The remainder of this chapter will constitute a brief overview and discussion of Evelyn Underhill's classification of transformation by way of five stages as described at greater length in her classic, *Mysticism: A Study in the Nature and Development of Man's Spiritual Consciousness*.

First, it is critical to note that Underhill herself cautioned against viewing these stages mechanistically or linearly as if they always and in all cases perfectly described transformation of consciousness in the literal way a map of London, for example, described London. When a particular mystic's transformation is examined, for instance, discrete stages with perfect boundaries most often cannot be identified. Vast variances, such as the overlapping of stages, reversal of their usual order, even the skipping of stages altogether is the rule rather than the exception. Underhill thus refers to the five stages as representing a "composite picture" involving considerable individual diversity.

So, while considering Underhill's work, instead of criticizing its more minute points, it might be more salutary to ask ourselves a key, overarching question: Can the quite specifically Christian mysticism of Underhill – and, by extension, any western model – possibly inform or support non-dual understandings of spirituality and, indeed, of reality?

The first of the five stages Underhill terms "awakening." Usually sudden, the individual experiences release, relief and great joy as if a weight has been taken off her shoulders.

Interestingly, "awakening," as Underhill uses this term, seems identical with what Abraham Maslow, decades later, would refer to as "peak experience." Based upon their research, Maslow and, more recently, Andrew Greeley, have claimed that peak experiences actually occur, at least occasionally, to most people.[1]

Underhill refers to the second stage of spiritual transformation as "purgation," a stage during which ego is reduced or, as has been discussed elsewhere in this text, "de-centered" as a "new center," is created by the "rising up" of consciousness or awareness.

Moreover, Underhill regarded this evolution from awakening to purgation as the initiation of "the mystic way" and to those relatively few who leave stage one and enter upon it as seeking earnestly to be cleansed from everything and everybody which they view as obstructing "God's will" from being done in their lives.

It is also the purgative experience which triggers many of us to seek religious or secular counsel, an endeavor Jung, for one, believed could be helpful, provided the counselor was at least somewhat further along than the counselee on the mystic path. Unfortunately, the purgative stage has very frequently been viewed by professional helpers as representing psychological pathology rather than spiritual progress.[2]

Underhill's stage three is called "illumination," and the imagery of light, recalling as it does the term "enlightenment" itself, carries with it the connotation of the individual's now being able to see more clearly as the darkness of unconsciousness is dispelled. There is also inferred here a process of liberation from deeply conditioned patterns of thought, emotion and behavior. Stage three, says Underhill, is often a time of happiness following upon the rigors of purgation. This is a stage, moreover, beyond which even many of those who started out on the mystic way never pass.

Next, for those ready, able and willing to move beyond illumination, comes what St. John of the Cross termed "the dark night of the soul" and what other mystics have called "the mystic death" or "spiritual purification." Once again, as is true of stage two, stage four is often pathologized by medicine and psychology as "clinical depression." This stage has also been referred to as "the desert," during which the light of illumination seems to have disappeared.

Stage four is generally interpreted as a "weaning" of consciousness away from false dependencies and entanglements, including the dependency upon the experience of exuberance during illumination. Christian mystics have described this stage as characterized by an acute sense of God's absence.

Finally, according to Underhill, comes "union," in which one's will becomes fully aligned with God's will, or, as it is sometimes put, falls away altogether and is entirely replaced by God's will. Jung referred to this phenomenon as "the mystic marriage." Other mystics have used terms such as "deification" and "unitive consciousness" to describe it. St. Paul, in his Letter to the Galatians (2:20), states "…it is no longer I who live, but Christ who lives in me." In the experienced certainty of deep connection to the divine, consciousness is finally at peace.

---

[1] See the appendix of this book for Maslow's listing of the common characteristics of peak experiences.

[2] See, for example, John E. Nelson's book, *Healing the Split: Integrating Spirit into Our Understanding of the Mentally Ill*; 1994.

※

Chapter 33

A Non-Dual Response to the Claims
of Western Mysticism

It should be noted, at this point, that Underhill and others, when discussing union, or an identification with the ultimate or God, were careful to distinguish this phenomenon from what they sometimes referred to as "pantheism" or as "an Asian absorption into the one." In this qualification, she was, as have been the great majority of Christian, Jewish and Islamic mystics, concerned with remaining within the western theistic tradition, avoiding heresy and any suggestion that "human will" and "God's will" are, or ever can be, identical.

But is this distinction between human and divine a real, ontological distinction? This is the central question posed, I believe, by non-dualists, especially perhaps to those raised in western cultures. Given the question's critical nature, I will provide here a brief response to it. In so doing, my hope is that I am articulating the concerns of many readers.

The first issue which, of course, must be met head on is the question of the nature of reality. As I treat this central issue, the stray logical positivist or materialist who may have, perhaps against his inclinations, actually read this far in my presentation will find much to criticize. But I must approach the issue of what is "really real" as a mystic and a non-dualist and cannot, given the nature of this text, discuss philosophical perspectives that run far afield from the text's basic thrust.[1]

Thus it is that we must ask two questions: "What is the human self?" and "What is the Ultimate (or God, the Divine, Brahman, Tao, the Self, etc.)"? The reader will by now know my own answer to both questions: The terms "human self" and "divine" point to the same non-dual, transcendent reality (which we have most often in this text called the Self), which cannot be captured by reason. If so, then the same principle is true of all other dualisms: self/other, I/you, this/that, here/there/ light/darkness, up/down, good/evil, etc.

In short, the true ultimate includes all opposites and itself has no opposite. This true ultimate cannot be fully described by any word (including the word "ultimate") – "cannot be spoken of," as the first line in the Tao te Ching, puts it – because it is the very act of speaking. Or, to put it somewhat differently, the true ultimate is the one and universal speaker or actor.

Who or what, then, is it that seeks? And what is the seeker seeking?

For the traditional western mystic, the answer seems quite simple: The seeker is me and I seek God. But, as shown above, for the non-dualist the possibility of this western dualism has been foreclosed by the non-dual claim that all opposites are ultimately two aspects of the same reality or process. The non-dualist must, in short, answer: Seeker and sought are one. They represent the terms of language, abstractions or, as Joseph Campbell put it, the "masks of God," their unity veiled by human thought and language.[2]

I, then, am not merely seeking God? I actually *am* God? Once again, the issue of identity comes immediately to the fore and misunderstanding is a certainty unless we fully comprehend the implications of the non-dual claim.

For the pronoun "I," from the non-dual level, itself must be understood as not referring to a person – Karl, for instance. "I," instead, ultimately refers to that level which cannot be named or objectified and which includes all opposites – in short, "I" refers, in the first person, to the same dimension as does the word "God" in the third person. They are two terms that, from differing angles, refer to who and what we are – the one Self.

Thus it is that Jesus says in the gospel of St. John: "I and the Father are one." The pronoun "I," here, no more refers to the man, Jesus of Nazareth, than it does to human role of Karl Galten, which the Self is playing in the drama. Indeed, "I" refers here to my, and your, ultimate identity, the Self itself.

The above claim has been discussed elsewhere in this text. Here, though, we must add another dimension to it. We must take up the issue spoken of so extensively over many millennia by countless mystics and seekers of all types and from all cultures and which today draws such persons to read books such as this one: The issue to which I refer, of course, is that of spiritual transformation.

The previous chapter constituted an overview of a particular "mapping" of the stages experienced by the seeker/mystic as she undergoes transformation. But what if the self which would undergo transformation is but a mind-made abstraction and thus not actually real or even existent? And what of that which accomplishes the transformation? Alas, it seems we stand on the edge of a thoroughgoing re-conceptualization of the issue.

After all, if what *does* the transforming and that which *is transformed* – a pair of opposites – is ultimately one, how can we speak of stages, which, of course, seems to pre-suppose a separate human self which exists in time and space and which "goes through" these stages? Moreover, as also discussed elsewhere in the present text, if there truly are no boundaries anywhere in the universe, then time itself is an illusion and all form exists in an unchanging now. What implications does this truth have for the issue of spiritual progress?

I believe the answer lies between the extremes of fundamentalism on both the western and non-dual sides as we view the issue experientially and non-dogmatically. If ever the expression "both/and" applies, it is certainly here.

Those of us interested in non-duality, after all, make the claim that the Self is *both* the formless witness *and* the infinite array of forms that are witnessed. Similarly, the Self is both "asleep" in form and "always awake," both the actor and the parts played, both voluntarily estranged from itself and never for a moment separated from itself.

Moreover, we *celebrate* this truth, and see no need to shrink from the fact that ultimate truth is thus unknowable by the discursive mind, cannot be captured by words and, though we value the human capacity for reason, we hold that reason falls short of grasping the mystery of non-duality.

So why wouldn't we accept, at a strictly relative level, that many earnest seekers have discerned "stages" or "phases" of spiritual growth (though, ultimately, there are neither stages nor seekers), continue to speak of the grace of God (though "God" refers to my own ultimate identity) or continue to pray (though the one praying is the one being prayed to)?

These views, assertions and practices are, after all, attempts to describe or to capture largely indescribable experience and mythological constructs rather than ontological statements or descriptions of the nature of reality (though, it must be acknowledged, many believers do not distinguish between description of experience and attempts to describe reality). So we need not be iconoclastic here. In fact, we, like the gnostics of the first three centuries of the Christian era, may even find real meaning in metaphor and not be any less non-dual.

At the same time, when the need for metaphysical description arises, we need not hesitate to point to the realm of the ultimate, formless and unnamable, the ground of being and to identify ourselves, and all form, with it. If, as Alfred North Whitehead said, "Christianity is a religion looking for a metaphysic and Buddhism is a metaphysic looking for a religion," we are free to enjoy the relative pointers to truth that the best in the world's religions have provided us while, simultaneously, knowing the ultimate truth that we ourselves, in our supreme identity as the Self, *are* that truth.

This knowledge is the omega point of consciousness, whatever metaphors we may find helpful or to whatever extent we may eschew all metaphor.

---

[1] For an excellent discussion of this issue, see Alan Watts' article "The Language of Metaphysical Experience" in the book *Become What You Are* (1955) edited by Mark Watts.

[2] Campbell, Joseph (1991). *The Masks of God*, volumes 1-4.

✿

Conclusion

It is my sincere hope that the preceding chapters have functioned to promote the expansion of consciousness in you. But there is no need to evaluate your mental or emotional states as verifications as to whether or not this expansion has occurred. Emotional and mental states, after all, come and go and are, contrary to popular assumption, ultimately of no absolute importance. As stated and implied in this text many times, one's conscious awareness of the eternal and underlying awareness in the present moment – or now – is the only ultimately important experience in this life; nothing else is of ultimate importance as everything else exists in the realm of form. The overriding purpose of this book, then, has been to introduce the reader to – or to make her more intimately acquainted with – the deepest aspect of her very Self.

If you believe that this objective has been essentially met, then the way ahead is clear: You are free, in any and all circumstances and at any time or place, to simply be aware of awareness. This is neither a prescription nor a method; it is a fact of your existence. So, as I say to so many clients, I say to you: You may go slowly. A step at a time. And keep doing what you're doing.

Yes, ego, along with whatever pain remains in you, will attempt pushing itself to the center. This need not be viewed as a problem and can simply be noticed and witnessed. There is no imperative to fight or to resist ego or your shadow; they will continue to gradually fade away, and have undoubtedly already faded considerably.

This book, moreover, has provided ego with no role whatsoever in the enlightenment process and so you may, at times, even hear ego saying "This book was fine. But it didn't provide me any tools or methods." Ego, in other words, however much it becomes, and has become, marginalized, is not likely to give up its main refrain, which goes something like: "But how do I get this?" Ego can be counted on, in other words, to continue insisting that enlightenment is, or should be, its own project. No problem. No action need be taken against ego when it says this. The deep Self knows the truth. We are free to let it take care of everything.

There is only this, only now. And that is all that is ever needed. You will become more and more comfortable with the utter simplicity of this truth and in the experience of the present moment. You are clean, free, and enjoy the privilege of direct and unmediated access to the ground of being. In turn, the light of the ground, as it becomes less and less obstructed by the person, will shine forth with all the more purity and brightness. That is a promise.

You are becoming transparent to the very ground of being. You are free to witness this phenomenon as it happens by, through and in you.

I will ask one final time: Could anything be better than this?

✤

Appendix

There is no better source among recent psychologically-oriented writers than Abraham Maslow when exploring mystical phenomena. Maslow proposed the term "peak experience" to refer to the "intrinsic core, the essence, the universal nucleus of every known high religion…"He understood peak experiences, furthermore, to be revelatory in nature and used the terms mystical, ecstatic, transcendent, and peak experience interchangeably.

In his study of peak experiences, Maslow found the latter to variously manifest at least 25 characteristics. They include the following: [1]

1. The universe is experienced as an organic whole.

2. The subject experiences intense concentration

3. There is a sense of detachment.

4. The subject experiences desirelessness.

5. The experience is self-validating.

6. It is an end in itself.

7. There is a sense of eternity and transcendence of space.

8. The world is seen as good and beautiful.

9. The subject feels charity toward all entities.

10. He experiences an intuition that all entities are sacred.

11. She believes herself to be a passive receiver of the experience.

12. There is a sense of awe, reverence, humility and surrender.

13. All polarities are transcended.

14. There is an absence of fear or anxiety.

15. The subject experiences an intuition that there exists a parallel world - a "heaven" - around us.

16. He accepts his uniqueness.

17. There is a sense of profound freedom.

18. The subject experiences a feeling of selflessness.

19. A loving and accepting attitude pervades the personality.

20. The self is viewed more psychically and less an object of the physical world.

21. There is a lack of selfish striving.

22. The dichotomy between pride and humility is transcended.

23. There is an impression that the sacred can be seen in the worldly.

24. The experience often has therapeutic aftereffects upon the personality.

25. There is a belief that one has been given a gift of grace.

---

[1] Maslow, Abraham (1964). *Religions, Values and Peak Experiences,* p. 19.

❁

Bibliography

Adyashanti (2011) *Falling Into Grace: Insights on the End of Suffering.* Sounds True Publishing.

Alcoholics Anonymous (2001). Alcoholics Anonymous World Services, NYC.

Arraj. J. (1986) *Christian Mysticism in the Light of Jungian Psychology: St. John of the Cross and Dr. C.G. Jung.* Chiloquin, OR. 97624: Inner Growth Books.

Assagioli, Roberto (1991). *Transpersonal Development: The Dimension beyond Psychosynthesis.* Thorsons Publishing, San Francisco.

Campbell, Joseph (1991). *The Masks of God* (volumes 1-4); Arkana Publishing.

Canda, E. (1991) East/west philosophical synthesis in transpersonal theory. *Journal of Sociology and Social Welfare,* 18(4), 137-152.

Cassel, R. (1990) Transpersonal psychology as the basis for health care. *Psychology: A Journal of Human Behavior,* 27(1), 33-38.

Chopra, D. (1989) *Quantum Healing: Exploring the Frontiers of Mind/Body Medicine.* New York: Bantam Books.

Cummings, C. (1991) *Ecospirituality: Towards a Reverent Life.*
New York City: Paulist Press.

De Mello, Anthony (1992). *Awareness: The Perils and
Opportunities of Reality.* Doubleday, NYC.

Deutsch, Elliot (1973). *Advaita Vedanta.* University of Hawaii
Press, Honolulu.

Firman, J. and Vargiu, J. (1980) Personal and transpersonal
growth: The perspective of psychosynthesis. In Boorstein, S.
(Ed.) *Transpersonal Psychotherapy.* Palo Alto, CA.: Science and
Behavior Books.

Foote, W. (1987) A case of transpersonal visualization. *Journal
of Transpersonal Psychology,* 20(1), 29-35.

Foster, Jeff (2007). *Beyond Awakening: The End of the Spiritual
Search. Non-Duality Press.* Salisbury, United Kingdom.

Gelderloos, P., Walton, K., Orme-Johnson, D., & Alexander, C.
(1991) Effectiveness of the transcendental meditation program
in preventing and treating substance misuse: A review. *The
International Journal of the Addictions,* 26(3), 293-325.

Gill, Nathan. (2004) *Already Awake: Dialogues with Nathan
Gill.* Non-Duality Press; Salisbury, United Kingdom.

Godlaski, T. (1988) Transpersonal psychology and the
addicted experience. *Alcoholism Treatment Quarterly,* 5 (3-4),
245-256.

Greven, John (2005) *Oneness: The Destination You Never Left.* Non-Duality Press; Salisbury, United Kingdom.

Grof, S. and C. Grof (Eds.) *Spiritual Emergency: When Personal Transformation Becomes a Crisis.* Los Angeles: Jeremy P. Tarcher, Inc.

Grof, C. & S. Grof (1990) *The Stormy Search for the Self.* Los Angeles: Jeremy P. Tarcher, Inc.

Hartong, Leo (2007) *Awakening to the Dream: The Gift of Lucid Living.* Non-Duality Press. Salisbury, United Kingdom.

Hawkins, David R. (2011) *Dissolving the Ego, Realizing the Self: Contemplations from the Teachings of David R. Hawkins;* edited by Scot Jeffrey; NYC and London: Hay House.

James, William (1958) *The Varieties of Religious Experience.* NYC: The New American Library.

Jung, Carl. (1958) *Psychology and Religion: West and East.* New York: Pantheon.

Krystal, S. & Zweben, J. (1989) The use of visualization as a means of integrating the spiritual dimension into treatment: II. Working with emotions. *Journal of Substance Abuse Treatment,* 6(4), 223-228.

Lajoie, D. & Shapiro, S. (1992) Definition of transpersonal psychology: The first twenty-three years. *Journal of Transpersonal Psychology,* 24(1), 79-98.

Liquorman, Wayne (2004). *Never Mind: A Journey into Non-Duality*. Advaita Press. Redondo Beach, CA.

Lukoff, D. & Lu, F. (1988) Transpersonal psychology research review topic: Mystical experience. *Journal of Transpersonal Psychology*, 20(2), 161-184.

Lukoff, D. (1988) Transpersonal perspectives on manic psychosis: Creative, visionary, and mystical states. *Journal of Transpersonal Psychology*, 20(2), 111-139.

Maslow, A. (1964) *Religions, Values, and Peak Experiences.* Columbus: Ohio State University Press.

Matos, L. (1991) The roots of depression in a suicidal crisis: A transpersonal approach. *Journal of Indian Psychology*, 9(1-2), 24-35.

May, Herbert and Bruce Metzger (Eds.) (1973) *The New Oxford Annotated Bible, Revised Standard Version.* Oxford University Press, NYC.

Mooji (2014) *White Fire: Spiritual Insights and Teachings of Advaita Zen Master Mooji.* Mooji Media

Muzika, E. (1990) Evolution, emptiness, and the fantasy self. *Journal of Humanistic Psychology*, (30), 89-108.

Myers, L. (1988) *Understanding an Afrocentric Worldview.* Dubuque: Kendall/Hurt.

Nelson, John E. (1994) *Healing the Split: Integrating Spirit into Our Understanding of the Mentally Ill.* State University of New York Press, Albany, NY.

Nelson, P. (1990) The technology of the praeternatural: An empirically-based model of transpersonal experiences. *Journal of Transpersonal Psychology*, 22(1), 35-50.

Otto, Rudolph (1958) *The Idea of the Holy.* Oxford University Press, London.

Peoples, K. (1991) The ego revisited: Understanding and transcending narcissism. *Journal of Humanistic Psychology*, 31(4), 32-52.

Plaskow & Christ (Eds.) (1989) *Weaving the Visions.* San Francisco: Harper and Row.

Rosenthal, J. (1990) The meditative therapist. *The Family Therapy Networker*, 14(5), 38-41, 70-71.

Small, J. (1981) *Becoming Naturally Therapeutic: A Return to the True Essence of Helping.* New York: Bantam Books.

Small, J. (1987) Spiritual emergence and addiction: A transpersonal approach to alcoholism and drug abuse counseling. *ReVision*, 10(2), 23-36.

Spira, Rupert (2008) *The Transparency of Things: Contemplating the Nature of Experience.* Non-Duality Press. Salisbury, United Kingdom.

Sutich, A. (1980) Transpersonal psychotherapy: History and definition. In Boorstein, S. (Ed.) *Transpersonal Psychotherapy.* Palo Alto, CA.: Science and Behavior Books.

Sylvester, Richard (2005). *I Hope You Die Soon: Words on Non-Duality.* Non-Duality Press; Salisbury, United Kingdom.

That Which You are Seeking is Causing You to Seek (1990) Mountain View, CA.: A Center for the Practice of Zen Buddhist Meditation.

Tillich, P. (1967) *My Search for Absolutes.* New York: Simon and Schuster.

Underhill, Evelyn. (1911) *Mysticism: A Study in the Nature and Development of Man's Spiritual Consciousness.* London: Methuen and Co.

Underhill, Evelyn (1942) *Fruits of the Spirit –Light of Christ – Abba.* NYC, Toronto: Longmans, Green and Co.

Underhill, Evelyn (1955) *Mysticism.* New York City: Meridian Books.

Waite, Dennis (2003) *The Book of One: The Spiritual Path of Advaita.* Winchester, UK: O Books.

Walsh, R. & Vaughn, F. (1980) Comparative models of the person and psychotherapy. In Boorstein, S. (Ed.) *Transpersonal Psychotherapy.* Palo Alto, CA.: Science and Behavior Books.

Walsh, R. (1992) The search for synthesis: Transpersonal psychology and the meeting of east and west, psychology and religion, personal, and transpersonal. *Journal of Humanistic Psychology*, 32(1), 19-45.

Watts, A. (1951) *The Wisdom of Insecurity*. New York: Vintage Books.

Watts, Alan (1972). *The Supreme Identity: An Essay on Oriental Metaphysic and the Christian Religion*. Vintage Books, NYC.

Watts, A. (1974a) *Cloud-Hidden, Whereabouts Unknown*. New York City: Vintage Books.

Watts, A. (1974b) *The Essence of Alan Watts*. Millbrae, CA: Celestial Arts.

Watts, Alan (1989) *The Way of Zen*. NYC: Vintage Books.

Watts, Mark (Ed.) (1995) *Become What You Are*. Lond and Bostom: Shambhala Books.

Weinhold, B. & Hendricks, G. (1993) *Counseling and Psychotherapy: A Transpersonal Approach*. Denver: Love Publishing Co.

Wheeler, John (2012) *Full Stop! The Gateway to Present Perfection*. Salisbury, United Kingdom: Non-Duality Press.

Wheeler, John (2007) *You were Never Born*. Salisbury, United Kingdom: Non-Duality Press.

Wilber, Ken (1977) *The Spectrum of Consciousness*. Wheaton, IL: The Theosophical Publishing House.

Wilber, Ken (1981) *No Boundary: Eastern and Western Approaches to Personal Growth*. Boston and London: Shambhala Publishing.

Williamson, R. & Farrer, C. (Eds.) (1992) *Earth and Sky: Visions of the Cosmos in Native American Folklore*. Albuquerque: University of New Mexico Press.

Wolinsky, S. (1991) *Trances People Live*. Falls Village, CT: The Bramble Co.

Yutang, L. (1948) *The Wisdom of Laotse*. New York: Random House.

Zukav, G. (1979) *The Dancing Wu Li Masters*. New York City: Bantam Books.

About the Author

Transformation of consciousness began in Thomas Galten by way of recovery from alcoholism, a compulsive condition which Tom has since come to regard as a bellwether, as are all compulsions, for deep-level inner shifts.

Since the arrival of this new dimension of awareness, Tom has studied a wide variety of religions, psychologies and philosophies, research which has strongly influenced his practice of psychotherapy and teaching, professions for which he is formally trained and which he continues to practice.

But it is Tom's own inwardly experienced and ongoing renewal, begun in acute suffering and enriched by his exploration of the mysticism which appears in many settings, guises and disciplines, that continues to fascinate and engage him. It also inspires him to pass on to others, through both the written and spoken word, the esoteric knowledge that has been given to him.

Thomas Galten lives in Milwaukee with his wife and daughter.

New from River Sanctuary Publishing

God Is: Ending Hell with a Course in Miracles, by George Provost. 2017. $18.95

Sundances: Prose Poems, memoir by William Climbing Sun. 2017. $12.95

A Curious Pebble: the Hollow Earth and Pursuit of the Holy Lance. A novel by David DiPietro Weiss and Danny L. Weiss. 2017. $16.95

The Journey of One, a memoir of awakening, by Jenifer Marie. 2017 $14.95

Dreaming the Light, full color art and poetry, by Melanie Gendron. 2017. $14.95

Getting There: Journeys and Learnings in the Dance of Life, a memoir by Annie Elizabeth Porter, 2016. $16.95

Favorites

From Illness to Stillnes: Uncovering Your Innermost Being, by Michael S. Harrington, CMT, NCCAOM, 2015. $13.95

Love, Alba (a novel), by former NY Times bestselling author Sophy Burnham, 2015. $15.95

A Goddess Journal, (blank journal with illustrations and affirmations) by Melanie Gendron and Annie Elizabeth, 2015. $12.95

River Sanctuary Publishing
P.O. Box 1561
Felton, California 95018
www.riversanctuarypublishing.com
(831) 335-7283

We offer custom book design and production with worldwide availability through print-on-demand, with personalized service and author-favorable terms. Specializing in inspirational, spiritual and self-help books, biography, and memoirs, full color art books.